In a

Stable

CW00481557

Christmas plays
for carol services

Imogen Clout

Published in 2014 by FeedARead.com Publishing

A CIP catalogue record for this title is available from the British Library.

Churches and other organisations may reproduce plays in this volume for performance purposes provided that there is no charge made to an audience or congregation. In any other circumstances permission should first be sought from the author: imogen.clout@btinternet.com; Twitter: @imogen_clout
Please, in each case, acknowledge authorship.

I would also be grateful if you would let me know if you stage one of these plays, and would welcome feedback.

Contents

		Page
Introduction		9
Notes on how to stage these plays		14
1.	What the Animals Saw	19
2.	On the Road to Bethlehem	25
3.	All out of Darkness we have Light	35
4.	We Hear the Christmas Angels	45
5.	The Gatekeepers	57
6.	The Angel Gabriel from Heaven Came	71
7.	There's Always Room	83
8.	When Christmas Comes	101
9.	Wait, Watch and Hope	121
10.	The Word, the Choice, the Birth	141
11.	Baboushka	155
12.	The Crib Set	171
Appendix: When Righteous Joseph wedded was		185

Joseph and me, we know what it feels
like to be sent by angels. So no
surprise, really, when in they came
that night, the hill men. Rough
but kind, they passed him round
like a lamb, kissed his brow,
tucked their great thumbs in his hand
and felt his tiny grip. They brought a cheese,
a fleece, a creel, and told of light
and singing and a voice. 'You won't believe…'
they said. 'O yes we will,' we said.
We too have heard and seen. We too
know how it feels.
We too.
We two.

Imogen Clout 2011

INTRODUCTION

All these plays were written for my church, St Andrew's Psalter Lane Church, Sheffield. They were written for our Christmas Eve Christingle Service. I have been very fortunate to have been allowed to write these services freely and creatively. For this I am very grateful to the two ministers in my time, Nick Jowett and Gareth Jones. I have also been very lucky to have an enthusiastic group of adults and children ready and willing to pitch in and act in the plays. Some of the children who started as tiny cherubs in these plays are now young adults and taking lead roles.

The Christingle Service at our church is by far the service with the largest congregation in the year. At many of these services we have had to fit in people with extra chairs in the Narthex, and even with people standing at the back and sides of the building.

It would be easy to dismiss this attendance as a non-religious hankering for sentimentality and nostalgia, a nod to a tradition that is dying. I think that it is something more, and springs from a hunger that people find it hard to voice. Going to church is now an unfamiliar experience for many people, and therefore off-putting, scary even. But at Christmas, and with your children, you may feel bolder and more comfortable. The carols are likely to be more familiar to you than the many hymns that are no longer part of regular school assembly. You may have some notion of what the story is about. So you come to church out of a set of mixed impulses, but you do come. It is a poor thing when clergy or regular churchgoers despise such motivation, and do not respond to the hunger that is there. If a Christmas service just trots out the regular readings and carols (often in a pallid imitation of King's College Chapel) and does not attempt to illuminate the significance of the events it commemorates,

9

or worse, presents a trite 'Nativity Play', poorly acted, and not very audible, this hunger will not be fed.

Crib tableaux and nativity plays have a long tradition and it is not hard to see why. The Christmas story is packed with dramatic scenes and visual imagery, reinforced by thousands of paintings. It is a story that calls to our imaginations. But its very familiarity means that for most of us it is not real; the characters in it are like the plaster crib figures. We are in danger of telling the story as though it begins 'Once upon a time".... That is, we treat it like a fairy tale (forgetting that such tales, too, hold powerful truths), set in a distant past, something suitable for children's ears that adults can listen to with sweet indulgence.

If we take this approach we are denying what theologians call *the scandal of particularity*, the problem that we may find in believing that God irrupted into history at a particular place and time in human form. We are behaving as though Jesus was not a real man. There are, to be sure, elements in the birth narratives in the Gospels that seem to contradict each other and mess up the chronology, and all the angels (let alone the idea of a Virgin Birth) may make it hard for some people to believe that this is how it happened, but this does not alter the fact that there was a human person called Jesus who was born and lived around this time in occupied Palestine. He had human parents too, with flesh and blood and emotions and sensibilities like other real humans, and there would have been other humans who were aware of his birth. The story is true, even if some of the factual elements may make us question it.

Such questioning and pondering is not wrong; it is the heart of what reading Scripture is about. We are invited to enter into the story, to place ourselves in the narrative, to imagine what it would be like as an unmarried teenage mother, or a respectable artisan, an elderly woman who has been barren all her life, a scholar who has travelled hundreds of miles. The task, at Christmas, is to make this come alive, to bring out the risk, and the scandal, and the sense of extraordinary events happening to people who think of themselves as ordinary, and the powerful sense of love and grace that illumines it. This does not happen to people in church often enough. I have lost count of the number of times people have made comments along the lines of: 'I never thought about how Mary/Joseph/other character would feel when....'.

You can only do this if you create in your drama people of flesh and blood, emotions and temper, inhibitions and reservations. Writing a play means that you have to enter into the scene and try to work out what might have happened. Novelists, and gospel writers can simply tell you, for instance, that an angel appeared to someone. The dramatist, unless the scene is going to be very dull, has to work out how this happened and what the mortal was doing at the time. You have to make precise choices: does the angel come in stage right or left, or running down the nave, or swinging in from the rafters? How is Mary to respond? What would you really say if someone strange suddenly came into your kitchen? Is she in the kitchen when it happens? The moment you allow yourself to flesh out the scene, it starts to come alive, and the crucial point of these dramas is to help your congregation realise that this really happened to real live humans, people like them, not characters in a story book.

My intention in writing these plays is not simply to tell the Christmas story again; I hope each year to be thought-provoking, to bring out some aspect of the story and its theology that may not have occurred to the congregation, or to give them a thought to take home

11

and return to later. For each play/service I have tried to find a *motif* or theme that will run through it, with echoes and repetition to reinforce it. This means that the drama may work on a number of different levels, giving pleasure (I hope) to those who are familiar with the story and its biblical context, and those who are hearing it as something new. For drama to be liturgical it also needs a rhythm and a measure of poetic utterance which wouldn't really work in a straight play.

The plays and scenes are only short, because the whole service is designed to take an hour. This means that I have not been able to explore some of the themes and issues in great depth. Inevitably there has had to be a bit of broad-brush-work, with shepherds and magi conforming to stereotype a little. It also means that mostly we have started the story with the Annunciation and left out Zechariah and Elizabeth and the Visitation. This is a great pity, because it gives the story greater depth and balance. There are many more things that could be said and explored if the format allowed.

My writing of liturgical plays owes a great debt to Dorothy L Sayers, who wrote a marvellous series of radio plays about the life of Christ, *The Man Born to be King*. These were broadcast during the Second World War, and had an extraordinary impact at the time. I discovered the book of plays when I was in my teens and it had a profound effect on my faith, making the gospel come alive for me in a way that has never left me. She taught me how to envisage a gospel scene and flesh it out while staying true to the characters involved. As well as the plays, the book contains a preface and the author's notes on performance that are full of theological insights. There are not many people alive now who remember the broadcasts and the plays seem to have been largely forgotten, which is a great pity. I have read and reread them over many years and am aware that there will be echoes of her dialogue in mine.

I also owe a great debt of love and gratitude to the Rector of my church when I was a child. The Reverend John Read always took the Junior Church himself and enlivened our Sunday mornings by getting us to act stories from Scripture. His embodiment of the Gospel, his great sweetness of temperament and his sense of the fun of the living word has stayed with me all my life. I hope that something of his spirit lives still in these plays.

You will see, if you read all these plays one after the other, that I have recycled material (and jokes) from one year to the next. Some years it has been hard to think up a new 'take' on the familiar story; sometimes the whole scenario has sprung into my head with an energy I can only attribute to the Holy Spirit, so little does it seem to have to do with my volition. It never ceases to amaze me, when a new idea comes. Truly, Scripture is the Living Word, an endless source of food for the journey.

Imogen Clout
Sheffield 2014

Notes on how to stage these plays
How the services work

The format of our Christingle service is a welcome, bidding prayer and responses, followed by a series of readings and Christmas carols interspersed with dramatic scenes. After the telling of the Christmas story the whole congregation comes up to see the Holy Family tableau, which has a real baby (borrowed for the occasion) and deposit their gifts for the Children's Society in the manger. They take a Christingle and return to their places. We light the candles, dim the lights, and the children sing Away in a Manger. We then welcome all the children who have been baptised and/or born during the year, (who have been specially invited to come to the service), have a brief set of prayers and end with a rousing carol and blessing.

In editing these plays for wider use I have omitted the bulk of our service, though where I wrote biddings and responses that picked up the theme of the play I have included them. The scenes in these plays can be used to make a stand alone play, or in a shorter Christmas service. I have included the readings and the carols that we used, but these are only suggestions. We have always tried to make the carols relate to the scene that they precede or follow. However, this does limit the choice because there are not many carols that are specifically about the shepherds or about the magi. I must confess to being heartily sick of 'While shepherds watched' but we have sung it now in a number of versions, including to the tune of 'Ilkley Moor' which is fun, or in the traditional Sheffield carol version called 'Sweet Bells', which has a delightful refrain between each verse that is easily picked up. 'See amid the winter's snow' is a good alternative, and has scope for the choir, or cast and the congregation singing different verses. There is also the lovely Isaac

Watts carol, 'Shepherds awake' which is unfamiliar to most people but can be sung to the tune of 'It came upon a midnight clear'. The magi pose similar problems; 'We three kings' is very popular but 'Brightest and best of the sons of the morning' has wonderful words and is well loved. 'In the bleak midwinter' also picks up the idea of bringing a gift to the manger and can be very moving at this point in the service.

When we have prepared these services I have always made the point to the cast that they are taking part in a piece of liturgy – it isn't just a play or a performance. The dramatic elements are there to illuminate, to amuse and console, but they are not there for an audience, but a participating congregation. So nobody has been required to learn his or her part by heart, and everyone has a script to hand, sometimes disguised with a prop. It is very helpful if everybody is really familiar with their part so that the pace of the scene works, but I would not want anyone to have the stress of worrying about forgetting lines.

Costumes

We have never made the costumes very elaborate. Shawls and headscarves for the women, with longish skirts, give enough of a period feel. Men can wear long gowns, but mostly we have used trousers and loose shirts, colourful cloaks (or dressing gowns) and hats for the magi and Barbour (or similar) jackets and wellingtons for the shepherds, with cloth caps. Sticks and staffs, baskets and bundles, can be useful props. Our angels of the smaller variety have had bare feet, oversized white t-shirts (bought very cheaply in the market) and a simple circle of tinsel. This makes them look quite adorable. For the children's version of the angel play we tie-dyed the t-shirts in amazing colours and the children gelled and spiked their hair with spray on colours – not conventional angels, but delightful. The Angel Gabriel in 2005 wore a white suit, bare feet, and a diamond earring and looked wonderfully unexpected, which helped the story. For the most recent play, The Crib Set, however, the story demanded that the characters looked like traditional plaster crib figures, so we were more conventional in our costumes, and Mary, for once, wore a blue robe.

Staging

We have always tried to keep this simple. One of the congregation is able to borrow two hay bales from a friendly farmer. These, suitably covered with army blankets or other rough cloth, give a suggestion of a stable. We try to remember that this is not a play, it is a service, so everyone is encouraged to have a script in their hand rather than learning dialogue by heart, although they should be thoroughly familiar with their lines. This helps with nerves. Audibility *is* an issue especially as the church is very full and not pin-drop quiet, so we use microphones as much as we can, and have on occasions used someone as 'mike-wrangler': their sole task being to move the radio mikes from actor to actor as scenes end.

Our church has a central dais at the point where the transepts meet the nave and chancel. Normally this is where the communion table stands, and this is where most of the action in these plays took place. The stable has often been behind this, in the chancel, but in recent years we have instead put it in one of the back rooms and taken the congregation through the back corridor which runs in an arc from one transept to the other behind the chancel. This gives a sense of journey and pilgrimage and means that the church is less congested as people move to the stable. In a more conventional church building you might use the space by the altar, or a lady chapel, to provide a similar space.

Readings

The readers need just as much rehearsal as the actors. It needs to be impressed on them that they must take time to 'tell' the story, even though it will be familiar to many of the congregation. For this reason, though I love the King James version and have it by heart after many years of listening to King's Nine Lessons and Carols on Christmas Eve, I have generally used other modern translations so that their unfamiliarity helps people to hear them afresh.

WHAT THE ANIMALS SAW
Christingle 1998

CAST	
Ox	*Other animals could be*
Donkey	*added in as well if you*
3 -5 Sheep	*wish, to make suitable*
3 Camels	*noises at various points*
Mary and Joseph	*Non speaking parts*

You can also add shepherds and wise men, non-speaking, for the tableau at the end.

NOTES

This, the first play that I wrote for Christingle, is the simplest and shortest of all the plays, suitable for a congregation of children.

The Ox wore a brown jumper and trousers and a straw hat with horns poking up through it. The Donkey had similar grey attire and a pair of ears on a hairband. Both spoke with local Yorkshire accents. The sheep all had big white t-shirts and dark glasses. The camels sounded really snooty and had costumes to suggest rich harness and trappings.

READING: **Luke 2, vv 1-5**
CAROL: *O little town of Bethlehem*

SCENE 1:

Ox   *(Comes in through the curtained door at the back.)*

The birds are going daft. They keep talking about this star. Too bright to get to sleep. They keep saying that something is going to happen.

I don't like things happening. I'm only a simple ox. I don't like change in my stable. Why can't it all be the way that it was?…..
That's what I should like to know.. *(Mumble mumble…..)*

Donkey   *(Donkey comes in from the side of the chancel. Doesn't see Ox at first. He is limping.)*

20

My feet…. ooh my poor aching feet.

Ox   Eh-up, Donkey. How do. Where d' you come from then?

Donkey   Nazareth. All the way from blooming Nazareth. And then all round Bethlehem trying to find a place to stay. And we've ended up in the stable, me *and* my people. It's not right. There's a baby about to be born, and him, master, going frantic about getting here and keeping her safe. She's going to have a baby, a very special baby. I could murder a carrot. Ooh, my poor feet. *(Moves over to the Ox and they both sit down.)*

READING: *Luke 2, vv 8 – 14 or 16 or 18*
CAROL: *While shepherds watched*

SCENE 2:
Ox: Make yourself comfortable, Donkey, and let's all try to get some sleep

(There can be five or more or fewer sheep. The lines can be distributed as appropriate. They come in from the back of the church in dark glasses, bleating as they come down the aisle. They speak with a bleating wobble.)

Sheep   -   Beeeh.
                   -   Help.
                   -   Thank goodness.
                   -   It was frightful.
              (Run into the chancel.)

Ox   Now then, what's this? Stop bleating.

21

Sheep	*(Subdued.)* Beeh.
Ox	Well? What do you think you're all doing here?
Sheep 1	We were on the hillside.
Sheep 2	We thought we saw an angel.
Sheep 3	It was too bright.
Sheep 4	It was too bright.
Sheep 5	It was too bright, man.
Sheep 1	It said there was a baby.
Sheep 2	A very special baby.
Sheep 3	Laid in a manger.
Sheep 4	In Bethlehem.
Sheep 5	It was very bright, man.
All sheep	It was very very bright.
Ox	Well, you can't stay here. We're full.
Donkey	That's my baby - it belongs to my people. You're in the right place!
Sheep 5	We're in the right place, man.
All sheep	We're in the right place. *(Bleat.)*
Ox	I'm never going to get any sleep. Stop your blethering. *(All animals sit down.)*
READING:	***Matthew 2, vv1 – 2, or 6, or 11 or 12***

SCENE 3:

(Camels come in in single file from the back jingling. Other animals stand up.)

Ox Camels!!???

Camel 1 We have come in search of a new born king.

Ox *(Heavily.)* Somehow that doesn't surprise me.

Camel 2 We have come from distant lands following a star.

Sheep 5 It's very bright, man.

All sheep *(Overlapping each other.)*
- Very bright.
- Very bright.
- Frightful.
-

Camel 3 I can't say it's what we had expected ending up here - but this is where the star has stopped.

Donkey It's my baby. What did I tell you? It's my baby.

Camel 1 But this baby, our masters say, is the Son of God.

All the animals Born in a stable!

23

Donkey   It's a very special baby! Didn't I tell you?

CAROL: *Silent night*
READING: *John I v 14 and 3 v 16*

During an appropriate lullaby carol the Holy Family (and other figures if you decide to have them) should take their places behind the screen. The screen itself should be moved just as the song finishes and the choir go back to their places. It can be folded up to the side of the altar in the corner.

The congregation come up to the stable to see Mary and Joseph and the baby, to present their gifts at the manger and receive a Christingle. The animals direct them.

ON THE ROAD TO BETHLEHEM
Christingle 1999

CAST	
Gabriel Angelos	*A news reporter*
Joseph	
Mary	
3 Shepherds	
3 Kings	

NOTES

This play needs a bit of technology to work properly – a camera linked to a projector with screen or a television screen so that the interviews are projected large.

As the congregation enter they see signs saying 'Bethlehem 3 miles" and finger posts pointing towards the front.

There should be a screen across at the front – perhaps across the chancel steps - with a door, which is meant to look like the entrance to a stable.

There should be an inn sign: "The Apple Tree".

At the very front of the seats there needs to be a seat for Gabriel and another for the camera-operator. (There should be a large screen at the front, linked to the video-camera.)

Suggested welcome and responses for this service:

Minister On this Christmas Eve, we welcome all travellers, all pilgrims, all strangers, all friends, as we meet at this point on the journey of life; as we pause briefly at the inn at Bethlehem to hear again the story of the coming of Jesus, of the word made flesh.

We join with the whole of creation in the joy, the wonder, the mystery of that night.

Minister	As we travel this road tonight
ALL	**Fill our hearts with joy.**
Minister	As we come to the humble stable
ALL	**Fill our hearts with wonder.**
Minister	As we kneel before the Christ Child
ALL	**Fill our hearts with peace.**
Minister	As we travel this road tonight and ever after
ALL	**Guide our footsteps on the way.**

CAROL:	***On Christmas night all Christians sing***
READING:	***Luke 2, vv 1-7***

SCENE 1:
Outside broadcast from the Bethlehem road.

(If possible for all these scenes, the lights should dim and the speakers should be videoed so that their faces can be seen up on the big screen. Gabriel should have a reporter's microphone to hold under the speakers' faces so that the words can be heard clearly. The lights should come back up at the end of the scene.)

Gabriel Good evening. This is Gabriel Angelos reporting for Sky television from the road to Bethlehem. I'm just outside the gates of the town. We have been hearing rumours - a story about to break. The town is heaving with people, all coming for the census. Everyone who was born here is having to return so that they can be counted by the Romans. All the hotels are packed out. I shouldn't think that there is a spare bed in the place.

27

(Joseph and Mary start to make their way down the aisle.)

Gabriel   Here come another couple of travellers.
We'll find out why they are here.
Excuse me, sir. Gabriel Angelos, reporting
for Sky Television. Why do you travel this
road tonight?

Joseph   We've come all the way from Nazareth
for the census. My wife's pregnant - she's
very near her time, so we had to take it
slowly.
(To Mary.) We're nearly there now, my
dear, and we'll find somewhere to stay.

Gabriel   I don't want to depress you, but there isn't
a bed to be had in the whole of town.

Mary   Oh, Joseph!

Gabriel   But I tell you what, if you go to the
landlord of the Apple Tree and mention
my name, he might be able to find you
room in the stable. It's clean - ish… and
it's got to be warmer than a night outside.

Mary   *(A little more desperately.)* Oh, Joseph!

Joseph   Thank you for your help. The Apple Tree,
you say? We'll try there then. Good night.

Gabriel   Goodnight.
This is Gabriel Angelos, handing you back
to the studio.

SCENE 2:

Gabriel   Welcome back.
The night is very cold now.
There have been some strange lights
up over the hills over there. As yet
we have no explanation.

(Shepherds and sheep start to come in from the back and down the aisle.)

Gabriel   But - there are some people coming
down the road from that direction...
people and .... animals.
Excuse me sir, Gabriel Angelos from
Sky Television.
Why do you travel this road tonight?

Shepherd 1   We've had a shock.
There we were, minding the sheep
(and our own business) and there was
a great light - like lightning, but it
went on and on - and a voice.

Shepherd 2   It was an angel - an angel saying that
the Saviour was born in Bethlehem
and we were to go and see him.

Shepherd 3   And we'd know when we found him
because it would be a baby all
wrapped up and lying in a manger...

29

Shepherd 1   And then there were hundreds of angels - you couldn't count how many - all singing, singing.

Shepherd 2   Singing Glory to God in the highest and peace to all people on earth.

Shepherd 1   So here we are - we had to come, you see.

Gabriel   That's a wonderful strange story. You might find what you seek at the Apple Tree Inn. There was a baby due to be born there tonight.

Shepherds   Thank you. Goodnight.

Gabriel   This is Gabriel Angelos, handing you back to the studio.

CAROL: *While shepherds watched*
READING: *Matthew 1 vv 1-12*

SCENE 3:
(During the last verse of the carol the star (a large helium balloon) is brought down the aisle by a gaggle of small angels and tethered in the chancel. Angels to sit down on the steps or floor of the chancel and look sweet.)

Gabriel   Welcome back. Even stranger things have happened since we were last on air. A huge bright star has moved across the heavens and now seems to be hanging over the town.

(Kings and retainers start to come in from the back and make their way down the aisle.)

Gabriel   And here come more travellers, rich by the looks of them, and foreign as well, I should say.
Good evening. Why do you travel this road tonight?

Kings   *(One after the other.)*
Good evening.
                    Good evening.
                                Good evening.

King 1   We are seeking a king.

Gabriel   In that case, perhaps you are on the wrong road. You'll find the king - Herod - in Jerusalem.

King 1   We have been there, but he is not the king that we seek.

King2   We seek a newborn king. We have seen his star in the east and have come to worship him.

King 3   When we asked at the court in Jerusalem the king called all his wise men to him and they said that your scriptures said that the baby would be born in Bethlehem. So we came here.

King 1   We have brought him gifts: gold....

King 2   and frankincense...

King 3   and myrrh.

Gabriel   That's the way to Bethlehem. I won't keep you. I should ask at the Apple Tree Inn. It all seems to be happening there tonight.

Kings   Goodnight.
           Goodnight.
                   Goodnight.

Gabriel   Gabriel Angelos, handing you back to the studio…..

CAROL: *'We three kings of Orient are'*
READING: *Matthew 2 vv 13 - 15a*

SCENE 4:

Gabriel   While we were off air I've seen the shepherds again, returning to their flocks, praising and glorifying God as they went. But the foreign travellers, they haven't been back this way. And there have been more developments: troops on the road, and messengers. I'm going to go on into the town and see what has happened. What have our travellers tonight seen? What miracle has happened in our little town?
If you want to know, you will have to make your own journey.
So, as I hand you back to the studio, I ask you this question:
What road will you travel tonight?

Minister   We invite you all to travel the Bethlehem road tonight and come into the stable to see for yourselves where the baby has been born.

Everyone comes up to the stable to see Mary and Joseph and the baby, to present their gifts at the manger [and receive a Christingle].

As the congregation go out, they will see on the back walls two large posters saying
WANTED
Have you seen this couple?
Reward for finding &c
and
WANTED
Have you seen these foreigners
Reward &c

ALL OUT OF DARKNESS WE HAVE LIGHT
Christingle 2001

CAST	
Anne	*Mary's mother*
Mary	
Joseph	
John	*3 shepherds*
Simon	
Mark	
Assorted cherubs	
Melchior	*3 wise men*
Caspar	
Balthazar	

NOTES

This Christingle was written for the Christmas after the 9/11 attacks. It seemed a difficult task to reflect on joy and hope after this. The theme of light even at the darkest hour seemed appropriate for the time.

This play requires Saint Anne to slap her daughter Mary – a quite shocking moment. You manage a stage slap by bringing your other hand sharply against your thigh to make the noise as you don't quite hit the other person's face. Or you have a colleague clap their hands at the precise moment. This needs a bit of rehearsal but it is very effective. Mary needs to react properly of course, bringing her hand up to her 'hurt' face. This completes the illusion.

We managed a wonderful theatrical moment at the beginning after the St John reading: someone dressed in black at the very front of the church lit an indoor sparkler that was tied on a sensibly long string to a dark coloured helium balloon and let it go. All the congregation could see was the sudden bright light ascending.

After congregation have arrived
Church in darkness
Reading: *John 1, vv 1-5 without introduction*

In the beginning was the Word, and the Word was with God and the Word was God. He was in the beginning with God; all things were made through him, and without him was not anything made that was made. In him was life, and the life was the light of men. The light shines in the darkness and the darkness has never blotted it out.

(Choir enter from back, down central aisle carrying candles or candle lanterns.)

Minister   On this Christmas Eve, we welcome you to the Christingle Service. In a dark world, on this dark evening, we remember the birth of Jesus, the light of the world, the hope of the despairing, the help of the helpless.
We give thanks for the birth of our Saviour, for the gift of God's humanity to us. We rejoice in the joy and hope that he brings us. We share again the glory of the first Christmas, when the angels sang and the wise men followed the star, to see the birth of the Prince of Peace.

Minister   In these times of war and trouble
ALL   **Come to our hearts O Prince of Peace.**
Minister   In the darkness of sorrow and loneliness
ALL   **Shine in our hearts, O Light of the World.**
Minister   In our homes and with our families this Christmas Eve
ALL   **Fill our hearts with peace and joy.**

CAROL   *'On Christmas night all Christians sing'*
READING   *Luke 1 vv 26-35, 38*
SCENE 1: In the house of St Anne

(The acting area should be pretty dark. Anne, obviously cross and bothered comes in – with a broom – she starts to take off her apron.)

37

Anne   (*Calling.*) Mary! Mary!
Where is that girl?
What's she up to now?
Mary!

Mary   (*Off stage. Calling.*) Yes mother?

Anne   Come here this instant!
(*Mary comes in with a basket of washing.*)
Now my girl, I want a word with you!
What do you think you've been up to?

Mary   Mother?

Anne   Don't you 'mother' me young lady. I rue the
day I bore you! What do you think you are
doing, bringing shame and disgrace on this
house?!

Mary   Mother! What do you mean?

Anne   You know full well what I mean! You've
fallen pregnant. And don't try to deny it. I
know all the signs. I ought to, the trouble
I've had with all of you!

Mary   Mother, you don't understand….

Anne   I understand enough to know that you've
betrayed my trust and insulted that good
man Joseph, when you should have made
him a decent and respectable wife. I've had
to tell him. I've sent him a message.
He'll be here any minute and you'll kneel
down and beg his pardon.

Mary   Oh. Mother, I haven't been bad. *He* said it would be all right....

Anne   You little... (*Slaps her face. Mary falls down crying. Enter Joseph, holding a lantern.*)

Joseph   Hello? Anyone there?
Oh Mother Anne, good evening. Goodness, whatever is the matter? Mary, my dear.
(*Goes to lift her up.*)

Mary   Joseph, oh Joseph, I'm so sorry, but it was an angel, you see, an angel, and he said that he came from God. What could I do? Of course I said yes.... And then the baby...

Joseph   Mary my dear, don't be afraid. I know what happened. The angel came to me too, last night, as I slept.
The Son of God, my dear!
Of course you said yes. And I will take care of you, and the baby when he comes, as long as live.
Mother Anne, we are all blessed.

Anne   I don't know what you two are blethering on about, but you're a good man Joseph, (even if you are a fool).

Mary   He's like a ray of light. Mother, mother, it's going to be all right, just like the angel said.

Anne   Angel! (*Laughs disbelievingly, but she draws them both into a warm embrace all the same.*)

(During the reading that follows, Joseph helps Mary on with a cloak, tenderly, and takes her on his arm, as they start to walk up the aisle to the back of the church.) Anne leans on the broom and waves as they go and then leaves by the side door.)

READING: *Luke 2 vv 1-5*

CAROL: *O little town of Bethlehem*

READING: *Luke 2, vv 8-14*

SCENE 2: On the cold hillside
(Simon is sitting on the ground with a very small lantern beside him, huddled up in his cloak. John enters with Mark behind him. They also have a lantern. All have long sticks/crooks.)

John   Simon, is that you?

Simon   It is. Who's that? Oh, John – and is that Mark you've got with you.

Mark   It is. How goes the night?

Simon   Perishing. I'm cold to my bones.

John   I hate this time of year. The wolves are fierce – hunger makes them desperate and bold. I heard them as we came up from the town.

Simon   The sheep are acting strange.

Mark   How d'you mean?

40

Simon	Huddled up like, nervous – like there's going to be an earthquake.
John	That's all we need. As if life up here wasn't hard enough at the best of times.
Mark	It's hard everywhere you go these days. Down there in Bethlehem it's heaving with people – all the inns full – folk sleeping in doorways, begging on street corners.
John	(*Chiming in.*) The prices are shocking and there are soldiers on every street corner - decent men and women insulted – bad times for everyone, you mark my words.
A voice	(*Calling out of the darkness.*) Shepherds, shepherds, Simon, John, Mark!
Shepherds All together	Who's that? Who called? Who is it?

(*A bright light as the voice continues:*)
Voice   Shepherds! Good news! Fear not!
God's son, the Messiah, the Christ, the
Holy one is born today, in Bethlehem.
Find him, shepherds!
In a manger! Wrapped in swaddling
clothes!
Go shepherds! Find the child of God!

(*As the voice has been speaking small angels have been*

41

*coming in at the sides and they line up across the chancel
steps. As the voice stops they start singing – then the
shepherds and then the choir join in.*
*We used the Taizé Gloria that goes in canon after the first
two bars, but you could use other music.*
*Then they take the shepherd by the hands and lead them
down the aisle singing it for the third time and getting the
congregation to join in.)*

**CAROL: (to the tune of 'It came upon a
midnight clear') 'Shepherds, rejoice! Lift up
your eyes'**

READING: *Matthew 2 vv. 1-2*

SCENE 3: In Balthazar's observatory
*(The three magi enter across the floor of the chancel making
for the pulpit (viewing platform). They carry lanterns.
Balthazar is leading the others. He is talking as though they
have been having a conversation outside.)*

Balthazar   …So I thought I must show the two of
you. It's the most remarkable thing I've
ever seen in my whole lifetime.

Caspar   I went back through the records after you
spoke to me. If it's as you say it's the
most remarkable thing since the records
began.

Balthazar   Come up my brothers, come up and see.
It is nearly time.

*(They climb the pulpit and shade their eyes to
look up to the back left hand of the church.)*

42

Melchior   You are right. My brothers! What a star.

Caspar   I never saw such a star, in such a conjunction!

Melchior   What does it mean?

Balthazar   The birth of a new king – a new kingdom.

Caspar   A new sort of kingdom – peace, my brothers – light in a dark world – love, heavenly love.

Melchior   The world has such need of this. All around us, war and conquest. People flee their homes – families lose each other – neighbours turn against each other. Oh we need the peace and love this king will bring.

Balthazar   We must go there – to Judea – for the conjunction clearly says that that is where the child is born – we must see this child.

Caspar   It's a long road, my brothers.

Melchior   But who could resist such a call. Such a star!

(They give it one last look as the carol starts and come down from the pulpit. As the music goes on they pull on cloaks, pick up staffs and packs, gifts &c and start to make their slow way up the aisle, looking up to the star from time to time as they go.)

CAROL: *We three kings of Orient are*

Minister   As light comes through the darkness and the baby is born in the stable we all rejoice. The shepherds are going to the stable. The wise men are going to the stable. Come with them to see the child.

Mary, Joseph and the baby appear in the stable (back altar).
Shepherds and kings and angels come back down the aisles following the star and act as stewards.
While congregation are coming to the manger:
O come, all ye faithful,
Choir remain seated and sing. (Congregation will join in as they can.)
The shepherds and kings finally gather round the stable.

WE HEAR THE CHRISTMAS ANGELS
Christingle 2002

CAST	
Michael	*Archangel*
Gabriel	*Archangel*
Raphael	*Archangel*
Assorted cherubs	*Bearing names of virtues – Grace, Joy, Mercy etc. You need 6 -8 or more*
Mary	*Non-speaking parts*
Joseph	
Shepherds	*3 or 4 shepherds who can sing*
Wise men	*Non-speaking parts*
Star carrier	*Non-speaking*

NOTES

This Christingle was written at the specific request of the church children who wanted a version of a play I had written for Advent ('Angels and Ministers of Grace') which gave them a real role; they also wanted to be 'punk angels'. They had the idea of tie-dying their white t-shirts all colours of the rainbow, and gelling their hair, preferably with colour and glitter so that they looked truly remarkable. This was very effective. As most of them were quite young – the oldest was 9 – I arranged the dialogue so that they could speak in groups. This made them both braver and louder.

The dramatic effect of the shepherds simply getting up from within the congregation was truly wonderful. We had four shepherds with good true singing voices and the effect of the two groups of voices was spine-tingling.

Minister   On this Christmas Eve, we welcome you to the Christingle Service.

We are gathered together as one family to give thanks for Christ's presence in the world.

We remember that all round us, unseen to our eyes, are the great crowd of witnesses, those who have gone before us and stand with us in the kingdom of Heaven. Tonight with them we raise our songs of praise.

We give thanks for the birth of our Saviour, for the gift of God's humanity to us. We rejoice in the joy and hope that he brings us. We share again the glory of the first Christmas, when the angels sang and the wise men followed the star, to see the birth of the Prince of Peace.

Minister	Open our hearts this Christmas Eve
ALL	**To hear the song the angels sing.**
Minister	When we are sad, or lost, or lonely
ALL	**Send us your messengers of light and love.**
Minister	In our homes and with our families this Christmas Eve
ALL	**Fill our hearts with peace and joy.**

CAROL: *On Christmas night all Christians sing*

SCENE 1: In heaven

(Angels' special operations room.
A sign to this effect should be held or hung up.
There should be lots of small angels milling around, and a couple of older ones, Gabriel and Raphael sitting in director's chairs reading the paper.
Enter the Archangel Michael with a clipboard. The older angels spring to attention.)

Gabriel	Squad!
	Cherubim!
	Ten-shun!
	(All the little angels line up across the front; this can be done with a fair amount of pushing and shoving.
	Number off, from the right.)

Small angels *(in order as they stand —add some more if you wish)*	Grace!
	Joy!
	Mercy!
	Peace!
	Love!
	Hope!

47

                        Faith!
                        Pity!

Michael   At ease.
                        Now, listen carefully.
                        The time we have all been waiting for is
                        at hand.
                        This is it! The fulcrum of history! The
                        pivot of creation! God becoming
                        human!

(Little angels bounce up and down going 'ooh!' and 'aah!'
and 'goodie!')

Michael   Now, now settle down. We've got a lot
                        to do. We've got to make sure that it
                        all happens properly. You know what
                        humans are like and how we have to
                        take care of them. The kingdom of
                        heaven is all round them, but they don't
                        always see it that way. They need a jolly
                        good shove to get it all right.
                        Now, first task. His mother – good girl,
                        recently engaged, name of Mary. She
                        needs the good news. And she's going
                        to hear it from us first. It'll be a bit of a
                        shock, so we need to break it gently.
                        She's only young.
                        Gabriel!

Gabriel   Sir!

Michael   You're good at this sort of thing. Pick
                        yourself a squad and go and do the
                        necessary.

Gabriel	Yessir!
Raphael	Sir?
Michael	Raphael?
Raphael	Sir. What about the fiancé, sir? Shouldn't we tell him too? It'll be an even bigger shock for him, I should think, sir.
Michael	Good thinking, seraph. You take that assignment. Pick a squad. He's called Joseph. Highly respected citizen. Make sure that he knows to treat her kindly. We're going to need a good dad for the future.
Gabriel & Raphael	Yes sir!
Gabriel	Right, you, you, you and you. Form up. Lead off. *(He exits with his squad.)*
Raphael	Right, the rest of you. Follow me. *(He takes his bunch off too.)*

READING: *Luke I vv 26-35, 38*

CAROL: *Long ago, prophets knew*
Christ would come, born a Jew

SCENE 2: In Bethlehem
(A sign to this effect should be held or hung up
The small angels Grace, Joy, Mercy, Peace, Love, and Hope

run in from all sides. They form a two-part speaking chorus.)

G J M	What are we going to do?
P L H	What are we going to do?
G J M	No room in the town!
P L H	The beds are all full!
G J M	Sleeping four to a bed!
P L H	No space to be had!
All	*(As Faith and Pity enter)* Where have you been?
Faith & Pity	We've found them somewhere
All the others	Where? Where?
Faith & Pity	At the sign of the Apple Tree
G,J,M	We looked there – no room!
F & P	Bet you didn't look in the stable!
G,J,M	Oh, not in there!
P,L,H	How mucky! How yucky!
F & P	No, lovely and warm. Lots of nice kind animals. We've filled up the manger with clean fresh straw.

	The inn-keeper's kind, and his wife will help with the baby.
G,J,M	*(As Mary and Joseph come in from the back.)*
	Watch out, here they come!
P,L,H	Quick! disguises, everyone!

(All the angels pull on coats and caps and woolly scarves etc. They split into two groups again with Faith and Pity joining one each.)

1	Welcome to Bethlehem
2	Have you come far?
1	Are you strangers here?
2	We'll show you the way.
1	The whole town's full up but we know where you can stay.
2	At the sign of the Apple Tree.
1	Come with us, it's not far now.
2	You'll be safe and warm and dry.

(The angels surround them lovingly and walk them to the back of the chancel where they sit down with their backs to the congregation and with a big cloak or blanket carefully wrapped round them.
The little angels sit to the sides and then join in the singing.)

READING: *Luke 2 vv1-5*

CAROL: *O little town of Bethlehem*

SCENE 3: Outside the town

(The small angels line up at the front of the stage. Enter to them Gabriel, a bit puffed.)

Gabriel   Now then, now then, now then. We can't have you lot hanging about like this. There's work to be done. People have got to be told. This isn't a secret arrangement. The kingdom of heaven is here. People must know. We've got to share God's marvellous good news.
We're off to the hills to tell the shepherds. Poor men, but honest folk.

(He lines the troupe up.
The shepherds have all this time been sitting about half way up the aisle. They stand up and move out to the centre facing the angels.
The next bit is all sung, to the tune 'Jesus Christ is risen today' - Easter Hymn. The congregation will be asked in the service sheet to join in with the last verse.)*

Shepherds	Hark the herald angels sing
Angels	Alleluia
Shepherds	Glory to the new born king
Angels	Alleluia
Shepherds	Peace on earth and mercy mild
Angels	Alleluia
Shepherds	God and sinners reconciled
Angels	Alleluia
Shepherds	Joyful all ye nations rise

---

* *This was one of the original tunes for the hymn, the first line of which was, originally, Hark, how all the welkin rings. You can hear a version on the Hyperion CD 'While Shepherds Watched*

Angels	Alleluia
Shepherds	Join the triumph of the skies
Angels	Alleluia
Shepherds	With the angelic host proclaim
Angels	Alleluia
Shepherds	Christ is born in Bethlehem
Angels	Alleluia
Shepherds	Hail the Heaven born prince of peace
Angels	Alleluia
Shepherds	Hail the Son of Righteousness
Angels	Alleluia
Shepherds	Light and life to all he brings
Angels	Alleluia
Shepherds	Risen with healing in his wings
Angels	Alleluia
All	Mild he lays his Glory by
Angels	Alleluia
All	Born that man no more may die
Angels	Alleluia
All	Born to raise the sons of earth
Angels	Alleluia
All	Born to give them second birth
Angels	Alleluia

(At the end of the singing the small angels run down the aisle to the shepherds, going:
'Come and see, come and see!' and take the shepherds up the aisle to where Mary and Joseph are still sitting with their backs to the congregation. They all group round and it could be at this point that the baby is handed over.
Gabriel should go off and the small angels sit down across the front of the stage in a row.)

READING: *Luke 2, vv 8-14*

CAROL: *'Shepherds, rejoice! lift up your eyes 'to the tune of 'It came upon a midnight clear'*

SCENE 4: *(Michael enters, still with clipboard, to confront the row of angels.)*

Michael   Well, well, well. Sitting down on the job. It doesn't stop there you know. We can't just tell the locals. This is God's gift to the whole of creation. Everybody's got to know.

(Enter Raphael, at a run.)

Raphael   's okay sir. Sorted. I've put the word out. There's a rather good star, if I do say so myself.

(Points to the back. Star comes in – small child with large helium balloon on long string. All small angels go ooh and aah and jump up and down.)

Michael   A star? What's it doing?

Raphael   Coming this way sir. With a following, if you see what I mean. Seers, wise men, sages, sir. That sort of egghead. They know what a star like that means, sir. Kingly birth, prince of peace, all that sort of stuff.

Michael   They can take the news to the whole world.

(Enter Gabriel at a run.)

54

Gabriel   Slight crisis sir. Bit of a problem.
                The wise men stopped off at Herod's
                palace, sir.
                He's asked them to go back to tell him
                where the baby is.
                If you ask me he's up to no good.

Michael   Well, we'll send them back by another
                way.
                After tonight, the whole world will have
                another way to go home by.

*(The star comes slowly down the aisle followed by the wise
men. The little angels form two speaking groups again.)*

1   Look at the star.

2   Look at the wise men.

1   Ooh look, they've got presents.

2   What do they bring?

1   Gold, a gift for a king.

2   Frankincense, a gift for a god.

1   And myrrh, a gift for a healer.

2   Our Lord; God, King and Physician!

1   How will they know where to go?

2   We'll tell the star.

1	Come and see the baby.
2	Come and see the baby.
1	This way.
2	This way.
1&2	*(To the congregation.)* You come too. You come too. This way. This way. Bring your gifts too. Bring your gifts too.

As everyone starts to come forward the holy family and the shepherds turn round and form a tableau with the wise men.
The choir sings: 'O come, all ye faithful'

This play, and the following one, are dedicated to the memory of Nick Wyatt, who played the Guard, Nathan, in this, and the Angel Gabriel in the 2005 Christingle. He was a very fine actor with a wonderful voice, who brought the characters to life. He died on 1st April 2014.

THE GATEKEEPERS
Christingle 2003

CAST	
Anna	*Innkeeper's wife*
Matthew	*Innkeeper*
Children of the inn	*4 or 5*
Guard 1, Nathan	*Old soldier, conscious of his authority*
Guard 2, Samuel	*Young and inexperienced*
Joseph	
Mary	
Shepherds	*Shepherd 1 and 2 have speaking roles. They should be able to sing lustily*
Wise men	*Only one has a speaking part*

NOTES

For this play we constructed a barrier for the town gate at the font, which stands at the back of the nave in the middle of the rows of chairs. We used a garden woven hurdle. The guards were there, and the inn was on the central dais.

The Guards should have pikes, or staffs of some sort, and a rough attempt at armour or uniform – breastplates and helmets if you can find some.

For this service I also used some of the Old Testament readings – on reflection I would now omit these as they made the service a little long for the younger members of the congregation. Voice I was up in the balcony, behind the congregation.

CAROL:	***Good Christian men rejoice!***
READING:	
Voice I	***Hear the word of the prophet Isaiah***
	Isaiah 40 vv 3-5

SCENE I: **At the inn in Bethlehem**

(Children entering with trays and brooms and other housekeeping paraphernalia to give the impression that the inn is full and they are very busy. The innkeeper should come in too and be on the dais directing operations.)

Innkeeper's wife (Anna)	*(Coming onto the dais from the side door which she has slammed.)* Goodbye and good riddance! Oh, it's too much, it's too much. Why do we have to put up with these wretched foreigners!

58

Innkeeper (Matthew)	Now, Anna, my dear, what's the matter?
Anna	Matthew, it's too much. I can't stand these filthy Romans. They can't keep their hands to themselves. Disgusting! Can't we just put up a sign saying 'No foreigners'? Why can't we just have our own kind here?
Matthew	No my dear, we can't, you know that. This inn is open to the whole world. Hospitality is important my dear. You know that it is God's commandment. Our forefather Abraham welcomed strangers to his tents, and it turned out that they were angels – you know the story – and they brought him and his wife untold blessings.
Children	Mother, don't cry.
Matthew	We must make everyone welcome. You know that, don't you children. Just as God welcomes us all to his world. Look at them all, packed in tonight. Not a spare room anywhere. There's one thing to be thankful for. If it wasn't for the Romans Bethlehem wouldn't be so busy tonight.

CAROL: *Long ago, prophets knew....*

(During the carol the family continue to move about, sweeping &c.
During the reading they move to one side so as not to be a distraction.)

READINGS:

Voice 1   *Isaiah 9 vv 6-7*

Voice 2   *Luke 2 vv 1- 5*

SCENE 2:

(The family come back up to the dais)

Matthew   Come my dear, come children. I think that we can all sit down and rest. The town gates closed an hour ago, There won't be anyone else turning up now. You've all worked hard tonight.

(Parents sit down on chairs and the children sit on the edge of the steps.
The scene then shifts to the back where the two town guards are seated one either side of the aisle. They will have dragged a hurdle across the gap during the carol.
Mary and Joseph come in through the back doors and knock on the barrier.)

Joseph   Hello! Is there anybody there? Hello! Can you let us in please?

(Guards get to their feet. Guard 1 is older, and rather pompous. Guard 2 is younger and not terribly quick on the uptake.)

Guard 1   Who's that?
What do you think you're doing, turning up this late? Respectable people

	are at home in their beds. The gate shuts at dusk. That's official.
Guard 2	That's right. You're too late. (*Aside.*) Riff-raff.
Joseph	Please. I beg you. Don't turn us away. We must find shelter tonight.
Guard 1	That's what they all say. The town council have entrusted us with the safety of honest citizens. That's our official duty!
Guard 2	That's right. No strangers after dark!
Mary	(*In a panicky voice.*) Oh, Joseph! I think it's starting!
Joseph	Please officer. Show us a little compassion. This is an emergency! It's my wife you see. She's (*whispers*) and it's our first. I don't think we've got much time.
Guard 1	Hwell! That does alter things. In the circumstances I think that I can exercise a bit of municipal discretion…
Guard 2	Do what?
Guard 1	….and authorize your entry. Samuel (*he pronounces it Sam – ewe –ell*) facilitate the procedure.

Guard 2   Do what?

Guard 1   (*wearily*) Pull back the gate.

Guard 2   But sarge…..you just said…

Guard 1   Just do it lad. You'll learn that you
                 sometimes need to 'interpret' the law.
                 (*Pulls back the gate.*)
                 And run up to the inn and see if your
                 sister can find them somewhere to stay.
                 The lady is… (*Whispers.*)

Guard 2   Oh! Oh yes sarge! Right away sarge.

*(He runs up the aisle to the inn and runs up to Anna and
starts to tell her waving behind him.)*

Guard 1   (*Who puts the hurdle back.*)
                 Now then, come on in, you two. The
                 town's packed to bursting with this
                 census. Follow Samuel there up to the
                 inn. Anna's got a sharp tongue but she's
                 a good heart.
*(They make their way up the aisle and the family come to
greet them.)*

Anna   Come in you poor things. You must be
                 worn out.
                 Matthew, where are we going to put
                 them? Every bed in the house is taken.

Child 1   Mother, there's still a bit of space in the
                 stable. We could move Balaam out into
                 the yard.

Child 2   And there's clean hay and straw in the loft.

Child 3   And I'll get some blankets from the chest.

Matthew   And I'll put the water on to boil.

Anna   Come on in.
(They go round to the back of the dais. If you can have a screen that they go behind this would be ideal.)

CAROL: *Child in the manger*
READINGS:
Voice 1   *Isaiah 40 vv 11-12*

Voice 2   *Luke 2 vv 8 - 14*

(There is a commotion at the back of the church as the shepherds enter in a slightly disorderly fashion but are brought up short by the shut gate. Guard 2 has returned during the carol.)

Guard 1   Oy! Who's that making a row? What do you think you're doing waking decent citizens in the middle of the night? Who are you anyway?

Shepherd 1   Don't stand on your high horse, Nathan. We all know who <u>you</u> are! (You're my sister's husband.) And you know who we are too! Honest shepherds the lot of us.

63

Guard 2   What have you done with the sheep?

Shepherd 1   Never mind about the sheep, man. Let us in; it's urgent!

Guard 1   Now, now Ben, you know the rules, same as I do. No entry after dark.

Shepherd 1   (*Mocking him back.*)
Now, now Nathan. Don't give us that! This is an…..(*Searches for the word*)…….EMERGENCY.

Guard 2   Not another one.

Shepherd 2   We've been sent, man. An angel told us…

Guard 2   An angel!

Shepherd 2   Yes, you daft lummock. The whole of the heavenly host, thousands of them, a whole skyful, singing like you've never heard.

Shepherd 1   It's true. They sent us down to find a baby in a manger – the new Messiah. Think of that you two. The Messiah, the Prince of Peace, come in our time! Now will you let us in?

Guard 2   A baby? A manger?

Shepherd 1   Look here, if you don't let us in, Nathan, I'll make sure my sister knows

where that wine jar went!
We've *got* to get in and find this baby.

Guard 1   Ahem! Well, if it's an angelic imperative
we're talking about.
Samuel, expedite the ingress!

Guard 2   Do what?

Guard 1   *(Wearily.)* Pull back the gate.

*(The shepherds come through the gate and start to sing.
As they sing the shepherds make their way up the aisle to the
inn.)*

CAROL:
Shepherds   See amid the winter's snow,
Born for us on earth below,
See, the tender lamb appears,
Promised from eternal years.

All   *Chorus*
Hail thou ever blessed morn!
Hail redemption's happy
dawn!
Sing through all Jerusalem:
Christ is born in Bethlehem!

People at   Say, ye holy shepherds, say,
the inn   What your joyful news today;
Wherefore have ye left your sheep
On the lonely mountain steep?

All   *Chorus*

Shepherds	As we watched at dead of night,
	Lo, we saw a wondrous light;
	Angels, singing peace on earth,
	Told us of Messiah's birth.'
All	*Chorus*

People at	Lo, within a manger lies
the inn	He who built the starry skies,
	He who, throned in height sublime,
	Sits amid the cherubim
All	*Chorus*

Sacred infant, all divine,
What a tender love was thine,
Thus to come from highest
bliss
Down to such a world as this.
Chorus

(The shepherds group round the back of the dais where the holy family are seated.)

READINGS
| **Voice 1** | *Isaiah 60 vv 1-3 and 6b and 19* |

| **Voice 2** | *Matthew 2 vv 1- 2 and 9b – 11* |

(Shine a bright light if possible to light up the inn.)

| **Guard 2** | It's gone awfully bright all of a sudden. |

| **Guard 1** | It's the star, Samuel. Hanging over the town like a great temple lamp. |

(Another commotion at the back of the church – jingling bells &c.)

Guard 1 Gracious heavens, you'd think this was Jerusalem, with the world and his wife turning up at all hours of the day and night and no rest for honest folks.
What's so special about Bethlehem, I should like to know?
Who goes there?

King 1 Travellers who come in peace, Master Warden.

Guard 2 Sounds like quality, Nathan.

Guard 1 Doesn't matter who they are, Samuel. You know the rules. More than my job's worth to let another lot in tonight and this lot look like foreigners to me.
We've had enough of their sort round here.
Sorry sir, we're not allowed to let anyone in after dark. By order, sir.

Guard 2 Yeah, by order.

King 1 Master Gatekeeper. We are no ordinary pilgrims. You see that great star there, hanging over your town – we have followed that star for hundreds of miles…

Guard 1 That's all very well, sir, but….

King 1 The star marks the birthplace of the

Prince of Peace, Master Warden. We
have come to worship him.

Guard 2   A prince, in Bethlehem, you must be
joking.

Guard 1   That'll do, young Samuel. We've nothing
to be ashamed of here. This is King
David's town, after all.

King 1   Master Warden, we beg your
compassion.
(There is a chink of coin.)
For the welfare of the poor, my good
man.

Guard 1   Well, sir, seeing as it's you. And it's a
matter of royalty….
Samuel, implement the access
procedures for these fine gentlemen.

Guard 2   You mean?….. pull back the gate?

Guard 1   Well done, lad, we'll make a sergeant of
you yet.

*(They pull back the gate and the kings progress up the aisle
to the inn.)*

Guard 2   Sarge, sarge, can we go too, sarge? To
see the baby, I mean. If he's all they say,
sarge, the Messiah, a Prince of Peace,
the gate'll be safe without us for half an
hour.

Guard 1   Well, lad…. I think you're right. If the Messiah is here, there'll be no need for gates and barriers any more.
What's more, I think we should tell everyone. After all, it's turning out to be no ordinary night.

CAROL   **Oh come all ye faithful**

Congregation come to the stable, ushered by the Guards.

THE ANGEL GABRIEL FROM HEAVEN CAME…
Christingle 2005

CAST	
Gabriel	*Archangel*
Zechariah	
Assorted cherubs	*If possible the smallest should carry the biggest instrument – a tuba or something similar*
Mary	
Anne	*Mary's mother*
Shepherds	*3 or 4 shepherds who can sing*
Wise men	*Non speaking parts*
Star carrier	

Notes:

This play owes a debt to the Iona Community's dramas printed in *Cloth for the Cradle*, an inspirational book.

I had already explored the theme of the angels as 'fixers', making sure that everything turned out all right, but how do people react to angels, and do angels get miffed if they are not believed?

In this play Gabriel ups the ante, so to speak, invoking more and more help to produce an impressive effect. We graded the troupe of cherubs by size, and the smallest, who had a disproportionate mass of curls, carried the largest brass instrument that we could borrow – to comic effect. The noise of the crash was pre-recorded.

Generally our choir has sat in the gallery at the back of the church for the service, as we tend to use every available seat for the congregation, but for this service they were at the back of the dais, so could leap to the feet, (in their choir robes) to add to the angelic heavenly chorus. Failing a choir, you could use recorded music.

Gabriel in this service, wore a white suit with his feet bare and a single glittering earring.

CAROL:　　*Angels, from the realms of glory,*
READING:　*Luke I vv 5 –23*

Scene I:　　In the Temple at Jerusalem

(There should be a small table, with something to hold the incense. You could use a thurible, if you have one, or a pierced metal tea light holder. Use incense cones if your church doesn't normally have incense. Zechariah comes onto the dais with a lighted taper. He lights the incense and puts his hands together in prayer. Gabriel comes onto the dais from behind him. He calls to him:)

Gabriel　　Zechariah! Zechariah!

Zechariah   Who's that? What do you think you're doing in here? Nobody's supposed to be in here – except me – that is. This is just for priests.

Gabriel   Zechariah.

Zechariah   And that's another thing. How do you know my name? I've never clapped eyes on you before.

Gabriel   Zechariah. I am the Lord's messenger, sent to you by God.

Zechariah   You're what?! This incense must be going to my head. God's messenger!
Don't be daft – you're not an angel.

Gabriel   Oh, but I am.
God has sent me to you with a very special message. You and your wife Elizabeth are going to have a baby.

Zechariah   There you go again – how do you know my wife's name? We can't have a baby. Don't be daft. We gave up all hope of that years ago. Far too old now.

Gabriel   *(Starting to lose his patience.)* Zechariah, I'm ashamed of you. Does all your priestly calling and study of scripture not show you that the Lord can do anything, particularly where the elderly prima gravida is concerned?

This baby will be the prophet for the Messiah, God's chosen one. You must call him John, and raise him carefully.

Zechariah   This has gone past a joke. I'll have to call the temple guards to remove you, I'm afraid.

Gabriel   (*Finally losing his patience.*) That does it! What's it going to take to convince you! You've been praying for this all your life, and when it happens you won't even believe your prayers have been answered! And you supposed to be a godly man. You'll be struck dumb! Now! And you won't be able to say a thing until the baby's born. That ought to convince you! There!

Zechariah   Mm mm….
(*They both go off in different directions off the dais. Zechariah should pick up the incense – but leave the table.*)

CAROL: *The angel Gabriel from heaven came,*
READING: *How the angel came to Mary Luke 1 26-38*
SCENE 2:   **In the kitchen at Mary's home**

(*Mary enters. Mary is wearing an apron and carrying a mixing bowl and a rolling pin, which she puts on the table. She starts to knead the contents of the bowl. Her mother, Anne comes into the kitchen. Anne is carrying a letter.*)

Anne   Guess what, Mary. Extraordinary news! Cousin Elizabeth is expecting a baby after all these years.

Mary   But mother, I thought she was too old.

Anne   It must be a miracle. God has answered her prayers at long last. But she says that Zechariah sees to have lost his powers of speech. It must be the shock! You'll have to go and pay her a visit.

Mary   I'll take her some things for the baby.

Anne   Yes. Oh dear. There's so much to be done, what with your wedding coming up too and all the things to think about. I'll go off to the market and leave you to get on with the baking.

Mary   Yes, mother.

(Anne goes out. Mary goes back to kneading. Gabriel, who is sitting at the end of the front row of the choir, stands up and addresses the cherubs who are sitting on the front row of chairs and at the feet of the ones on the chairs.)

Gabriel Now then, cherubs. *(They all stand up.)* After the last time, I may need a bit of back up. Just keep a low profile, but stand by if I call, okay?

Cherubs Yes, sir.

Gabriel Here goes. *(Strides onto dais.)* Mary!

Mary   Goodness gracious!
             Who are you? And what do you think
             you're doing in our kitchen?

Gabriel   Don't be afraid, Mary. I am an angel,
             God's messenger. I've been sent…

Mary   (*Interrupting.*) Yeah – really. I bet you say
             that to all the girls.

Gabriel   (*Sticking to his mission.*)..sent to tell you
             that you are going to have a baby.

Mary   (*Seizing the rolling pin.*) Well! I've heard
             some chat up lines in my time but…

Gabriel   Mary! Stop! I really am an angel. You are
             God's chosen one.

Mary   (*Beginning to be less sure of herself.*) Can
             you prove it? I though angels came with
             lots of cherubs.

Gabriel   Presto!(*Snaps fingers. The cherubs run out
             in two lines so that they are on both sides of
             the dais. Gabriel gestures to them.*)
             Cherubs.

Mary   I thought that they came with musical
             instruments.

Gabriel   Cherubs! (*They run back to their places
             and back round the dais bringing
             instruments. One of the smallest has a large*

brass instrument. As they take up their
places there is a large musical fanfare – the
equivalent of 'Ta-taa'.)
There! Angelic enough for you?

Mary   (Flustered.) I…..I…. How can he fly with
that thing?

Gabriel   (Takes her hands in his.) Mary. Listen to
me. This is important. God really has
chosen you. He wants you to be the
mother of his son, the Holy one, the
Messiah.

Mary   (Wails.) But I'm not married..

Gabriel   God's power can accomplish all things,
Mary. Have faith, child. All will be well.

Mary   (Kneeling.) I'm sorry. I've been foolish. I'm
sorry, I didn't believe you. I will do as he
wishes. I am God's servant.

Gabriel   (Raises her to her feet.) As am I. His
blessing be upon you.
Cherubs!
(They leave, Gabriel going first, moving up
the aisle to the font. The cherub with the
large instrument should go last.)

Mary   (Shading her eyes to watch them go.)
I still don't see how he can fly with that
thing.
(Noise of a crash.)

77

CAROL: *O little town of Bethlehem*
READING: *How the angel came to the shepherds: Luke 2, 1-16*

SCENE 3: On the hills above Bethlehem

(The three shepherds arrange themselves on the dais and appear to go to sleep. Gabriel and the cherubs are still round the font. Gabriel stands up.)

Gabriel   Right then. Now this time we're going to have none of that 'are you really an angel' nonsense. We're all going. Smarten up, all of you. Haloes polished. Wings unfurled. Instruments in tune… Off we go. Follow me.

(They march down the aisle and form up round the two sides of the dais facing inward. Gabriel proceeds right round to the back of the dais and enters behind the shepherds facing the main congregation. He spreads out his arms and speaks in awesome tones.)

Gabriel   Shepherds, awake!
(They do, rubbing their eyes in perplexity.)
Shepherds! Be not afraid! I bring you good tidings of great joy.

S1   What?

S2   Who do you think you are?

S3   Go on. You're having us on.

Gabriel   I am Gabriel, God's own messenger, an

78

angel from heaven. The Messiah has been born in Bethlehem. You will find him wrapped in swaddling clothes and lying in a manger.

S1 See here, mister. If you're the angel Gabriel, where's the bloomin' heavenly host?

Gabriel All round you, mortal. Can you not see?

(The shepherds look round and see the angels for the first time.)

S2 Blimey!

S3 It's a wonder it can fly with that thing.

S1 So why aren't they singing? I thought that's what angels were supposed to do.

(Climactic chord on organ. Whole choir leaps to feet. Enormous brief chorus – Glory to God, or Halleluiah or similar – do it with an amplified recording if necessary. Shepherds fall to their knees.)

Gabriel Now do you believe me!

Ss together Yes sir.
Sorry sir.
Certainly sir.

S1 Bethlehem, you say. Right away, sir.

S2 Come on lads; let's find this baby!

Gabriel	Cherubs!
	(They run round to the opposite sides of the dais and form up back in front of the choir)
S3	I don't know how he can fly with that thing.

(Crash.)

CAROL: *While shepherds watched/sweet bells*

READING: *How the angel came to the wise men: Matthew 2, 1-12*

SCENE 4: **While the wise men slept at Bethlehem**

(The three wise men come onto the dais and prepare for sleep. Gabriel, at the back of the dais stands up.)

Gabriel	Now then, cherubs, host, stand by. Any doubts, any 'you're not an angel' remarks – sock it to them, okay, full volume.
Cherubs and Choir	(Nodding.) Yes, sir.
Gabriel	(Moving forward onto the dais behind the wise men.)
	Caspar! Melchior! Balthazar!
	Hear my words and fear not.
	The Lord God has sent me to you.
	Do not trust the king, Herod.
	Do not obey his wishes.
	Conceal the hiding place of the baby, the Messiah.

80

	Preserve his life.
	Return to your country another way.
	(The wise men sit up.)

Caspar   Yes, Lord.

Melchior   We will, Lord.

Balthazar   We hear and obey.

Gabriel   *(Slightly taken aback.)* You do?

Balthazar   You are the Lord's messenger, how could we not?

Gabriel   It's true. I am. But that's not generally the response that I get.

(All the wise men kneel at Gabriel's feet.)

Caspar   We have seen the child.

Melchior   We have worshipped at his feet.

Balthazar   We know you come from God.

Gabriel   *(He raises his hand in blessing.)*
Blessings upon you. May your journey home be safe and swift. Fare well.

CHOIR   **Silent night**

During this carol the stable tableau comes together with Mary, Joseph and the baby in the centre, a basket at their feet for the offerings, the shepherds on one side and the wise men on the other.

THERE'S ALWAYS ROOM
Christingle 2006

CAST	
Keziah	*Innkeeper's wife*
Reuben	*Innkeeper*
Sarah	*Their children*
Jonathan	
Miriam	
Mary	
Anne	*Mary's mother*
Shepherds	*3 or 4 shepherds who can sing*
Wise men	*Non speaking parts*
Star carrier	

Notes

This Christingle had an extraordinary impact and lives long in the memory of the children who took part, partly because of the begging couple on the steps of the church. Many people were taken in by this and some refused alms with unkind words, or tutted about such a thing at a church on Christmas. Some were shamefaced when the couple revealed themselves. Others gave generously. Mary and Joseph collected nearly £40 before the service! The Magi — people dressed as Muslims sitting in the congregation - caused another frisson. Some people had refused to sit close to them.

This play has a slightly different format with a scene that takes place after the congregation have visited the stable. This covers the flight to Egypt and was very moving when it was first performed.

When people arrive they will see (but may not notice) a couple of beggars, male and female on the steps, with a crude cardboard sign reading:

HOMELESS
BABY ON WAY
PLEES HELP

They are Mary and Joseph.

There will also be a gang of layabouts (shepherds) passing a bottle and being mildly rowdy in the car park. Both of these groups will come into the back of the church when the service starts and sit in the Narthex.

The dais should have the altar table on it covered with a simple cloth. Behind it there should be two large straw bales. In front of it, two household chairs.

Minister   Welcome, everyone, to our Christingle Service.

Christmas Eve is here and once again

we come together to tell the story of Jesus' birth and bring our offerings for the work of the Children's Society. We will hear tonight how long ago a couple found a refuge far from their home, a baby was born in a stable, strangers and outcasts were told of his birth and travelled to see him, and then the family had to flee from persecution and seek asylum in a foreign land.

It's a story full of risk and danger; it's a story of love and hope. Out of this dark, fragile beginning, comes Jesus, the light of the world.

Minister	May the light of the stable welcome us in
ALL	**So we may come to worship with generous and loving hearts.**
Minister	May the light of the star guide our paths
ALL	**So we may follow and find our hearts' salvation.**
Minister	May Jesus, Light of the World, shine in our lives
ALL	**So we may reflect his glory to the whole world.**

CAROL:	***On Christmas night all Christians sing***
READING:	***The Angel Gabriel announces Jesus' birth: Luke 1, vv 26 - 37***

SCENE 1:   At the Sign of the Vineyard, an inn in Bethlehem

(Reuben, the innkeeper, comes on to the dais and sits down in one of the chairs. He stretches out his legs and puts a white handkerchief over his face and peacefully goes to sleep. He snores loudly.
His wife Keziah enters with a sheet of paper in her hand. She's in a tizz.)

Keziah   Husband!
Reuben!
Anyone would think this inn could run itself!
Wake up!

Reuben   *(Peacefully.)*
Yes, dear?
What is it dear?

Keziah   This. *(Brandishes paper.)*
Another Roman decree! That Caesar Augustus! ! He wants to count everybody! As if we didn't have enough to do! Who does he think he is?

Reuben   *(Mildly.)* The Emperor, dear. Count everybody?

Keziah   Everybody. Well, all the men. They've all got to back to their home towns. Bethlehem will be packed out.

Reuben   When, dear?

Keziah   Six months time, in the winter. At least we've got a bit of notice.

| | But there's no time to lose; we've got to get cracking if we're going to be ready for all the extra customers.
Fetch the children and the servants. |
| --- | --- |
| **Reuben** | Yes, dear. (*He goes off to the side; meanwhile Keziah is visibly making lists, ticking things off on her fingers. The children/servants run in and sit on the dais at the parents' feet.*) |
| **Keziah** | Now listen, all of you. In December Bethlehem's going to be full to bursting with people coming for the census. We've got a lot of work to do to get ready. You know our motto – "There's always room at the Vineyard." We've got to make sure it happens, and we need to start now. Sarah. |
| **Sarah** | Yes, mother? |
| **Keziah** | You're in charge of blankets and mattresses. Start counting and mending, and ordering more from the weavers if we need them. |
| **Sarah** | Yes, mother. (*Goes out, taking one or two smaller children with her.*) |
| **Keziah** | Jonathan. |
| **Jonathan** | Yes, missus? |
| **Keziah** | The whole place needs a good whitewash, |

	especially the stable. You and David and Simon. You get started on that.
Jonathan	Yes, missus. (*Goes out taking one or two with him.*)
Keziah	Miriam.
Miriam	Yes, mother?
Keziah	We need to start getting the food supplies in and drying and bottling everything that we can. There's flour to order and raisins and figs, jars of olives, and all the meat from the butchers. We must make sure that there's enough for everyone who comes. We've never given short measure at the Vineyard. Take the others with you and start going through the stores.
Miriam	Yes, mother. (*She goes out with the others.*)
Keziah	Reuben.
Reuben	Yes, dear?
Keziah	I need you to order the wine, dear. At least six of those big jars I should think. Goodness me, so much to do. If the king himself came down from his big gold palace in Jerusalem I'd want the Vineyard to be ready to welcome him.
Reuben	Yes, dear. (*They go off the dais to the side.*)

CAROL   *Long ago, prophets knew*

READING   *Mary and Joseph come to*
Bethlehem
Luke 2, 1-7

SCENE 2:   At the sign of the Vineyard

(No one is on the dais at the start.
Keziah comes in taking off her apron, trailed by Reuben and
the children.)

Keziah   Well, that's it. I think we're just about
done. We can all sit down and have a well-
earned drink.

Reuben   Yes, dear.

Children,   - I don't think I've ever seen so many
one after   customers.
the other   - The place is packed – every room full.
- The fattened calves went down a treat.
- Lucky you ordered so much in, mother.

Keziah   Well, I think we've coped. It's been a bit
tight in places, but no-one's likely to come
now. The town gates shut an hour ago.
Now, what about that drink.

(A child starts to pass round cups and pour drink. While this
goes on, Mary and Joseph come in from the back of the
church. They get to the back of the pews, and Joseph
speaks:)

Joseph   Come on, dear heart. Only a little farther.
There it is now, the Vineyard. They said it
was a good big place.

89

(He comes up to the edge of the dais and knocks with his staff on the edge. The family look up at the sound and Sarah goes to the door.)

Joseph   Good evening. I wonder… do you have any room.

Sarah   No, sorry, we're full up. It's the census.

Joseph   We've been all over town…. Are you sure you can't find us anywhere? My wife, you see, she's very near her time.

Sarah   Every room's taken.

Keziah   (*Calling.*) Who is it, Sarah?

Sarah   Some people, mother. They want a room.

Keziah   (*Coming to the door.*) I'm very sorry sir…

Sarah   Mother (*Whispers in her ear.*)

Keziah   Oh…. so I see. Well… there's always room at the Vineyard. That's our motto. But as it is we're all pushed out of our own rooms, and the children are in the hayloft.

Sarah   The stable, mother!

Keziah   The stable. What a good thing we whitewashed it!
The corner near the manger! Quick everyone.

90

> *(Dishing out tasks as they come.)*
> - mattresses
> - a brazier
> - blankets
> - soup
> Reuben – boil some water – quick as you can

Reuben   Yes, dear.

Keziah   Now you two, you come with me. We'll make you as snug and warm as we can. Don't you worry my dear, I've eight of my own.

> *(Leads them round the dais to the back where they can sit amid the hay bales with their backs to the congregation for the time being.) Everyone else goes off to the side for the moment, but should come back to the dais in the last verse of the next carol.)*

CAROL: *God rest you merry gentlemen*

READINGS   *The Shepherds are told the news of Jesus' birth: Luke 2, 8-16*
The wise men follow the star: Matthew 2, 1-12 (or put this reading later – see note p.94.)

SCENE 3:   **At the sign of the Vineyard**

(All is quiet in the inn. The children are sleeping peacefully on the floor of the dais. Mary and Joseph are sleeping at the back with their backs to the congregation. Keziah and Reuben come in from opposite sides. She is wiping her hands on her apron.)

Reuben   Is all well, dear?

Keziah　　　It is, husband. A fine baby boy. Although it's her first and she's just a slip of a girl, they're both doing fine.

Reuben　　　You come and sit down dear, we could both do with a bit of rest.

Keziah　　　It's hardly worth going to bed. It's a lovely night. I've never seen a winter sky so bright.

Reuben　　　And so quiet, so still. Peace over all the earth.

(They pause for a moment looking up at the sky. The peace is rudely shattered by an eruption of the shepherds who come through from the Narthex singing Torches, and carrying torches and lanterns. They should sound very merry and noisy.)

Shepherds　Torches, torches, run with torches
(singing)　　All the way to Bethlehem.
　　　　　　　Christ is born and now lies sleeping.
　　　　　　　Come and sing your song to him.
　　　　　　　Sing my friends, and make you merry.
　　　　　　　Joy and mirth and joy again.
　　　　　　　Lo, he lives, the King of Heaven,
　　　　　　　Now and evermore. Amen[*]

Reuben　　　What the....?

Keziah　　　What on earth!? *(Addresses the shepherds, who have come to a slightly swaying stop at*

---

[*] *You can find this in the Oxford Book of Carols, (pub OUP) both the new and old editions.*

the edge of the dais.)

What do you think that you are up to coming into town making a noise like that? I won't have you waking my guests. This is a respectable house, not a four-ale bar.
Reuben, make them move on.

Reuben   Yes, dear.

Shep 1   Now look here, missus. We've come to see the baby.

Keziah   The baby? What baby? How do you know about the baby?

Shep 1   So there is a baby. Just like he said. In the stable?

Keziah   The stable! How do you know about the stable?

Shep 1.   Aha! You see, missus, we've had a whatdoyoucallit.. a thingummy…a hoojamaflip..

Shep 2   A messenger.

All the small shepherds   An angel!
An angel!

Keziah & Reuben   An angel?

93

A t SS	And all the heavenly host.
Keziah	It's shameful, letting the young ones drink like that.
Shep 1	We're not drunk, missus. Not with wine anyway. We were told to come and find the baby.
AtSS	The angel said he'd be in the manger.
Shep 1	He's the one, missus. The Messiah. The one who's to save us all.
Shep 2	The hope of hopes.
Shep 3	The Saviour of Israel.
Keziah	In our inn? In our stable?
AtSS	Yes. Yes. Please can we see him, please?
Reuben	I'll show you the way. This way lads.

(*They all follow him round the back, where they need to sit down round the Holy Family and keep still for the next bit. Keziah sits down rather heavily and dozes off.*

YOU COULD PUT THE MATTHEW READING IN AT THIS POINT, AND HAVE THE STAR WALK IN DURING IT.

The star arrives either: dangled over the balcony, or as a helium balloon, on the end of a string walked down the aisle by at least one and possibly several small cherubs. It should be attached to a weight (so it doesn't get lost in the rafters if

a cherub loses hold of it!) and the cherub should place the weight on the table and then go round to the back too.
As the star arrives figures should get up from various places in the congregation and make their way to the central aisle. They should be dressed so they look 'foreign' – there should be a veiled woman for instance, or men in shalwar kameez and skullcaps. One or two should have walking staffs.
They come up to the dais and one of them knocks on the dais with the stick. Keziah wakes up. She goes to the 'door'.)

Keziah   Who is it? Who are you? It's the middle of the night.

Wise Man We are seekers, madam. We have
1   followed the star.

Keziah   Star. What star? *(He points and she does a double take.)* Oh. *That* star. Where did that come from?

WM1   From heaven, madam. It has led us to your door.

WM2   It tells of a great birth, of a new born king.

WM1   The king of kings, madam.
                Tell us where we may find this child.

Keziah   Where have you come from? You're not from round here, by the looks of you.

WM2   We have travelled a long way to see this child.

Keziah   You aren't the only ones. Shepherds. Foreigners. Well, there's always room at the Vineyard (that's my motto) – and he's a lovely baby. You'd best come in. They're in the stable.

WM1   The stable, madam? This is a kingly birth!

Keziah   Well, no-one thought to tell me at the time. There wasn't a spare bed in the house. If King Herod himself had come, he'd have had to sleep in the stable.

WM2   It may yet happen, madam. The palace sent us here.

Keziah   The palace. Goodness gracious. You *had* better come in. And the rest of the household had better get up.

(Turns and claps her hands calling 'Get up! Get up!' And leads the wise men round the back of the dais.)

Prayer - invitation to baptism families. Coming to the manger as we sing: The First Nowell followed *by* Christingle prayer, then Away In A Manger

(During Away in the Manger the stable tableau should dismantle: shepherds should go to the lectern side of the dais and sit down, the wise men to the other side. Mary should remain in the stable with Joseph. The little angels can

96

be asleep there too. The inn children should come to the other side of the table and be asleep on the floor. Reuben and Keziah should take one of the chairs each and be asleep.)

The lights are switched on again and the Christingle candles are put out

SCENE 4:   At the sign of the Vineyard
(Joseph and Wise Man I come onto the dais, each carrying a lantern.)

Joseph	Landlord! Reuben!
WM I	Madam! Keziah!
K & R	*(Waking.)* What is it! Who's there?
Joseph	I'm sorry to wake you.
WM I	And I.
Joseph	But I've had a dream.
WM I	And I too. I have had a dream.
Joseph	A warning.
WM I	And I! A warning angel.
Joseph	Herod!
WM I	Yes! The king!
Joseph	He's going to kill the baby!

97

WM I   Soldiers are coming!

Joseph   We have to get away!

Keziah   O no! O my goodness! What are we
                going to do? Reuben! Reuben!
                Do something!

Reuben   Yes, dear.
                (He suddenly becomes very decisive.)
                Wake the children! Pack some food!
                Get the shepherds – they'll know the
                paths into the hills.

Keziah   Where will they go? What will they do?

Joseph   Egypt. That's what my dream said.
                We'll seek asylum there.

Reuben   Yes, dear. Egypt. Herod won't be able
                to touch them there.
                Hurry dear, there's no time to lose.

Keziah   *(Unexpectedly meek.)* Yes, dear.

*(They wake everyone up. There is bustle and fuss. The
shepherds come round to the front of the dais. The Holy
Family group at the front of the dais. The wise men remain
on the right. All the family and the angels line up on stage.)*

Reuben   Now, go safely and quickly. We'll do what
                we can here to cover your tracks.

WM I   We will go home by another way to lead
                them off the scent.

Shep I   We'll see you safely through the hills.

Keziah   (*Embracing Mary.*) God go with you my
              dear, and remember, if you every make it
              back to these parts (*whole family joins in*)
              there's always room at the Vineyard.

(The shepherds go slowly up the aisle with Mary, Joseph and the baby. At the third verse the wise men go out to the back of the transept. Everyone on the stage sings, as they wave goodbye, to the tune Quem Pastores.)

**Go, go safely, leave the manger,
Flee the soldiers and the danger,
Wander in the world a stranger,
Go, go safely, Holy Child.**

**Bless us all who stand before you,
We are joyful that we saw you
All God's creatures here adore you,
Go, go safely, Holy Child.**

**Lord of every time and space,
Bless your children in this place,
Shed on us your heavenly grace,
Go, go safely, Holy Child.**

(The cast who are left on the dais move quietly to the sides)

WHEN CHRISTMAS COMES
Christingle 2007

CAST:

Vicar	Who can be male or female
Choir leader	
Peter	The young and callow Curate
Sarah	The server
Mrs Pargeter	Church worthy
Mother 1 – and her children	There can be up to 4 children to each mother
Alex	
Sam –	Another stressed parent, can be either sex
2 Men	
2 Homeless people	(Mary and Joseph)
Mother 2 - and her children	
Irene	An older lady from the sheltered housing near the church

Notes

This play was inspired by our construction of a new set of crib figures, which we used in the play. We used cheap artists' 'lay figures': those jointed wooden dolls that stand about a foot high. Various member of the congregation had dressed them in fabrics. (You could also use a set of knitted figures.) The various groups of the cast brought them in and so the crib was assembled.

The choir for this were up in the balcony gallery at the back of church, but you could easily position them in the chancel. If in your church, you call your vicar 'Father', you can substitute this where 'vicar' is used in the dialogue.

Our Vicar, Nick Jowett, very sportingly played the Vicar in the play, as well as being the minister leading the service. But you could use a separate actor and have another Minister for the service.

Minister   Welcome, everyone, to our Christingle Service.

Christmas Eve is here and once again we come together to tell the story of Jesus' birth.

In our busy world we sometimes find it hard to stop and listen, to hear the voice of God seeking our attention, to give attention to those who need our help, to give ourselves space and time so that we can speak of our deepest desires and the needs of our hearts.

Christmas brings us that peace, that time, that space: a moment of stillness in the middle of our lives when we remember again the complete and utter love that God has for us all, a love so great that God came to share our human existence.

Minister	After the seeking and the following
ALL	**Comes the answer and the truth.**
Minister	After the hustle and bustle of preparation
ALL	**Comes the calm and the stillness.**
Minister	After the waiting and the watching
ALL	**Comes the fulfilment of the promise.**
Minister	After the journey and the labour
ALL	**Comes the birth of hope and peace.**

CAROL: *In the bleak midwinter*

SCENE 1: The Vicar is upset

(The Vicar comes in in his cassock. He's got a clipboard and he's behaving a bit like the White Rabbit. He is plainly very agitated.)

Vicar	Oh dear, oh dear! Where is everyone? The Christmas Eve service starts in an hour and a half and nobody's here. *(Calls.)* Peter! Peter! Where's that curate of mine? Never there when you want him. I don't know what they teach them at theological college these days!
Choir leader	*(Leaning over the balcony.)* Was that all right, vicar?
Vicar	What? What's the matter?
Choir leader	I said, 'was that all right' – the carol –was that okay?

Vicar	It sounded fine to me – I wasn't really listening. I thought you were meant to rehearse earlier.
Choir leader	Sorry, vicar. We couldn't all get here in time. But we're all here now.
Vicar	Well you'll just have to fit in with everyone else. It's really most inconvenient. Peter!

(Peter comes in from the vestry at a rush. He's a bit rumpled and his hair is spiked and gelled in a way that you suspect that the Vicar disapproves of.)

Peter	Here, boss. Sorry, vicar. What's the matter?
Vicar	*(Spluttering.)* What's the matter! Christmas Eve! Our biggest service of the year and nothing ready. Where is everyone?
Peter	Have a heart, boss – sir* – vicar. Everyone's busy. There's all sorts of last minute things to do. Chill. They'll come. *(Sarah enters from the vestry, dressed in a server's alb.)* Look – Sarah's here now to get things sorted.
Sarah	Good evening. Hello, vicar. I'll start

---

* *You could use 'miss' if the vicar is female, as though Peter is still at school.*

getting things sorted out. I'll get the candles lighted soon. That'll make things feel Christmassy.

Vicar   There's so much to do, and no-one's here.

Peter   *(As Mrs Pargeter comes in at the back.)* Well, here's one. It would be her too.

Mrs Pargeter   *(Hurrying down the aisle, taking off her gloves but leaving her hat and coat on.)* Oh dear, Vicar, I'm so sorry to be late. I thought I had time. I was sitting there cutting crosses in the sprouts and then I thought I'd better peel the potatoes and then I thought about the stuffing and I thought I had just enough time to fit it in and then I couldn't find last year's Christmas pudding – the one that I made last year – and I was in the pantry and I suddenly looked at my watch and realised the time…..

Vicar   *(Impatiently.)* Yes, yes, Mrs P. Well you're here now. At least someone is, thank goodness. I don't know what we'd do without you. You'd better just run through your reading while we wait for the others.

Mrs P   Yes, Vicar. Where do you want me to stand?

Peter   Just here, at this mike please, Mrs P.

	(Sarah lights the altar candles as the reading begins.)
Mrs P	Saint Luke tells how the birth of Jesus was announced:
	Luke I vv 26 - 38
	Thanks be to God
	(Short pause at the end. Then the vicar nods.)

Vicar   Thank you, Mrs Pargeter. Very suitable.

(Mrs P goes to sit down in one of the seats at the side of the main aisle that has been reserved for her. There's a sort of scuffle as a woman comes in with a bunch of children (3-4). The children go to sit down on the floor to the side of the dais.)

Mother   Oh! Vicar! I'm sorry I'm late. I've brought the figures – the ones that I was making for the crib, but I had to go to see my mother in the home this morning and what with one thing and another I've been running late on myself all day. So here she is *(Unwrapping Mary.)* Oh! Where's the stable?

Vicar   *(Grimly.)* Where indeed? Peter? Where's it got to?

Peter   The guys who are making it said they'd have it ready in time. Relax. They'll be here. They're probably in the pub.

Vicar   *(In a despairing squeak.)* The pub!

Mother   *(Putting Mary on the altar to the left-hand side.)* Well, I'll put her here for the moment. She can sit and thing about what's going to happen. Poor girl, I don't envy her – far from here home and going into labour in a stable. Here's the angel *(Unwrapping him, and arranging him beside Mary on the altar as she talks.)* He knows, I think, how scary it all seems. Do you notice how he tells her not to be afraid. You might think an angel wouldn't worry about the way humans feel. You might think an angel would just say: "Tremble, mortal, and do what you're told". But he's kind to her and answers her questions. If you can call an angel 'kind'. Mind you, she's not just a passive creature, either. I'm not sure I'd have the nerve to question an angel like she does. There! *(She stands back to look at him.)*

Sarah   That's lovely. *(Mother goes to sit down.)*

Choir leader   *(Calling down.)* Can we do the next one, vicar?

Vicar   Yes, what is it?

Choir leader   The angel Gabriel from heaven came[*].

CAROL: *The angel Gabriel from heaven came*

---

[*] *Obviously (I hope) the choir leader calls down whichever carol you've decided on for each point in the service.*

107

SCENE 2:

(Another man has come in from the back and as the congregation settle down again, he comes forward.)

Alex   Hello, vicar. Sorry to be late. I had to get a last minute gift or two. Somehow there's always someone that I've forgotten. Sue sent me with Joseph – if you see what I mean. She's had to stay home. James is meant to be calling from Australia and she can't bear to miss him. She's finding it very hard with him away this year. Since Martin died, she's ever so much more protective of him – well, you understand…. *(He tails off, somewhat embarrassed.)*

Vicar   Yes, yes. Thank her for sending Joseph.

Alex   *(Unwrapping the figure.)* Here he is. Oh! Where's the stable?

Vicar   That's what we'd all like to know. I thought Peter had it all under control.

Peter   Chill. It'll be here.

Alex   I'll just put him here then. *(Puts the figure on the altar so that it is looking at Mary.)* There! He can look at Mary. Not much else he can do, poor bloke – someone else's baby wished on him. Still he must have brought him up kindly, so to speak. The kid turned out well, really. *(He stands back to look at the figures.)*

108

Do you know the poem about Joseph, Vicar? I found it the other day when Sue was sewing his cloak and thought you might like it. *(Fumbles in his pocket and brings out a folded paper.)* Here it is. *(Proceeds to read it out.)*

'I am Joseph, carpenter, ...'
(U.A. Fanthorpe's poem[*])
(Everyone stops to listen and there is a short, reverent silence. Then...)

Choir leader	Shall we do another one, vicar? When our God came to earth?

CAROL: ***When our God came to earth, not for him noble birth:***

(Alex takes a seat on the side of the aisle.
During this carol another party comes in all in hats, coats, gloves: an adult – Sam (can be male or female) - and some children, carrying the crates of Christingles.)

SCENE 3

Sam	I'm sorry to be so late, Vicar. First I dropped the keys under the car and then I couldn't get it to start, so me and the children had to walk – but we've managed to bring all the Christingles, even though it was a bit of a struggle. When would you like them.
Vicar	*(With a forced cheeriness.)* Oh, better

---

[*] *In Christmas Poems, by U.A. Fanthorpe, pub. Enitharmon Press and Peterloo Poets 2003*

late than never, hey. Over there.
(Waves to the tables at the left-hand side.)
Sarah will help you.

Sarah   *(To the children.)* That's lovely. Well
done. Can you bring them over here?
*(She takes them off to the side table and
they start setting them out.)*

Sam   Can I just run through my reading?

Vicar   Yes, You'd better.

Peter   You need to stand here. *(Shows him
where to stand.)*

Sam   The Birth of Jesus
Luke 2 vv 1 - 7
Thanks be to God

*(Enter from the back two men carrying the stable. The men
with the stable are just a little bit jolly, a bit 'whoopsadaisy'.
As they come in two other figures (the homeless couple)
follow them in a bit tentatively. Alex goes to speak to them,
they pause just past the font and have a conversation during
the next bit of dialogue.)*

Man 1   Here you are, vicar. Sorry to be late.

Man 2   Bet you'd begun to think that we'd
never make it.

Man 1   But here we are. Otherwise, it'd be a
disaster. First no room at the inn, then
no stable even.

Man 2	Where d'you want it? 'S bloomin' heavy!
Peter	Just here – on this table *(Indicating the round table in front of the altar.)* You've done a nice job.
Man 1	Glad you like it. Where's all the stuff?
Vicar	*(Alarmed.)* Stuff!?
Man 1	Yeah. People, animals, straw – that sort of thing.
Children with Mother 1	We've got that. Here it is. In the bag.
Alex	Excuse me, vicar. We need your help here.

(While Alex takes the Vicar up the aisle a little way to meet the couple who came in behind the stable, Peter and the children start to assemble the stable putting in the straw and the props and Mary and Joseph with the Angel. This needs to be done quietly and not distract too much from what is happening.)

Vicar	What is it? Can't it wait? We're rather tied up here at the moment.
Alex	It's like this, Vicar. These two say they're homeless. They were hoping to get

home to Hull* but there isn't a train now and they're looking for shelter. And the lad's been beaten up by some yobbos. His face is a mess……

Homeless man   We saw this was a church, right? And thought you helped people?

Homeless woman   So we came in. We're wet through and it's really cold. Can't we just stay here for a bit and get warm?

Mrs P   *(Weighing in as she gets up from her seat.)* Now look here. We've got a service starting very shortly. There'll be all sorts of people arriving – you see, don't you, you can't just stay here…

Vicar   *(Who may be harassed but is not having Mrs P rule the roost.)* Thank you, Mrs P. I'm sure we can find a bit of space, and some hot water….

Alex   I'll put the kettle on. You two come in the kitchen where it's warm and you can clean up that face and have a cup of tea. You don't need me just at the moment do you, Vicar?
I should think we've got some biscuits somewhere – you look as if you could so with a hot drink. *(As he steers them off to the back.)* That okay, vicar?

---

* *Substitute a suitable destination for your locality.*

112

Mrs P	Well, really! People who don't know how to behave! As if you can just turn up at a church on Christmas Eve! You'd better make sure that someone keeps an eye on the collection plate, Vicar.
Choir leader	What about another one, Vicar?
Vicar	Oh. Oh. Yes, fine. What is it?
Choir leader	While Shepherds Watched and Sweet Bells

(Children assemble on dais and sing together during carol. Another family arrive during this.)

CAROL: *While shepherds watched their flocks*

SCENE 4:

Vicar	Well, that sounded splendid. Now all we need is the shepherds. Peter, who was supposed to be getting them ready?
New family	We are! *(The children take them to Peter and help him to put them in the stable.)*
Mother 2	I'm sorry we're late, vicar.
Vicar	*(Gloomily.)* Everyone is. It's like herding cats this evening. How it's all going to be ready in time I don't know.

113

Mother 2   You've only got a service to organise! You try getting four children to wrap their parcels and write their Father Christmas letter and find the stockings and ice the cake and stuff the turkey and do a batch of mincepies, with your mother-in-law coming tomorrow to disapprove of everything – let alone making sure a bunch of shepherds are properly dressed. Men!*

Vicar   We've got less than an hour, and we're still hardly there. I'm still missing readers and crib figures. The stable's only just arrived. I thought Peter had it all under control. Everybody should have been here by now.

Mother 2   They will be. You're taking it all too much to heart.

Vicar   It's Christmas. How can you not take it to heart? The biggest service of the year! All those people coming to hear the story. It's got to be right.

Mother 2   What's still missing?

Vicar   The reader for the story of the shepherds. Annie was going to do it but I don't know where she's got to.

---

* *Sobstitute 'Vicars!' if the vicar is female, unless this is too near the knuckle!*

114

Mother 2	Don't worry. I'll stand in if she doesn't show up.
	Shall I just read it through now, in case? Kids, sit down and be quiet for a moment, will you?
	(She picks up a Bible and finds the place.) Here it is. I couldn't help thinking as we sewed the shepherds' clothes how they left everything, didn't they. Their whole livelihood there on the hills – and no certainty that it would all be there when they got back. They just get up and go. Sometimes it's a very appealing thought. *(Reads:)*
	Luke 2 vv 8 - 20
	Thanks be to God
Choir leader	Next one, vicar? See amid the winter's snow.
CAROL:	***See amid the winter's snow***
Peter	Okay, boss? Vicar? Nearly there now. Just the wise men to come, just like the story.
Alex	*(Coming down the aisle with a ladder.)* Gang way! Mind your backs!
Vicar	What on earth?
Alex	Star for the top of the tree, Vicar. And the lights. I nearly forgot. Got to have the tree lit up for Christingle.

(He sets up the ladder by the tree and with the help of the two Men fastens the star to the top and appears to be getting the lights to work. Meanwhile Sarah and a couple of the Christingle children take tapers and start to light the lights around the walls of the church.)

Vicar   *(To Peter.)* Who's doing the wise men?

Peter   A cooperative effort from the ladies from Southcroft*. I'll go and see if they're coming.
(Starts to go to the back to the church.)

Vicar   Well, they're not coming any distance. What's keeping them? *They* can't be stuffing the turkey!

Mrs P   *(Getting up from her seat.)* Shall I run across for you, Vicar?

Vicar   Mrs P. I wouldn't put you to the trouble. I'm sure they're on their way.

Mrs P   Oh it's no bother, I do assure you, Vicar.

Peter   *(Coming in with Irene, who has the wise men in a basket.)* Here she is!

Irene   Hello. Hello, vicar. Here we are. I've got the wise men all safe and sound. And the camel.

---

* Southcroft is the MHA care home next to our church; I suggest you use a suitable substitute local to you.

116

Vicar   What camel!

Irene   Well, they must have had a camel,
                mustn't they – coming all that way.
                Lots of camels probably. So he's a
                token camel so to speak. Maureen's
                grandson brought him all the way back
                from Dubai, so he's come a long way
                too.

*(She takes the wise men out of her basket and she and
Peter start to set them up in the stable.)*

Alex   *(From over by the tree as he switches the
                lights on.)* There you are, vicar, all up
                and running.

Peter   That's it, boss, vicar. All ready.
                Candles lit.
                Carols practised.
                Readings gone through.
                Stable all in place.

*(Everyone starts to gather round gently to see the stable
with gentle admiring noises. Even the homeless couple come
down the aisle to see. Then the Vicar suddenly pulls back
with a sort of startled shriek.)*

Vicar   Aah!

Mrs P and   What is it?
others   What's the matter?

Vicar   Where's the baby?

All	The baby?
Vicar	*(Spluttering.)* The baby! Where's the baby? Who was dressing the baby? We can't have a Christmas Service without the baby for heavens' sake! Why do you think we're all here?!!
Smallest child	I've got him in my pocket!
Vicar	Thank goodness. *(Calming down a bit.)* Can you bring him up? Would you like to put him in the manger? *(Child does so.)*
Peter	Now, boss, I think we're all ready.
Vicar	You know, I really do have a problem with your attitude about his. How can you be so laid back about it all? Don't you see it's all got to be right? You seem to think it will all happen by itself. And don't you dare tell me to chill, you cheeky young idiot. Where do you think the congregation are?
Mother 1	Vicar dear. [Edward.*] We're all here. Turn round and look. *(For the first time, the Vicar looks round and sees everybody there.)* It's all right. It's Christmas. You have to stop now and take a deep breath. Christmas won't come unless you give it the space to let it happen.

---

* *Substitute a suitable name – not your vicar's real name.*

118

Alex	She's right. We don't make Christmas happen, Vicar. God does that. But he can't do it unless we stop fretting and let it happen.
	In the stillness, in the pause: that's how He comes.

(There should be a moment of complete stillness and utter calm. Then the music starts and one by one the cast join in singing Silent Night.
At the beginning of the second verse, Sarah brings the Vicar's surplice and stole and leads him/her to his/her seat. The rest of the cast slowly divest themselves of their outer clothes and the children are revealed in white t-shirts and don tinsel rings for angels.
Peter and Alex lead the homeless couple to the stable where they become Mary and Joseph, surrounded by an adoring heavenly host.)

CAROL   ***Silent night, holy night***
(At the end of the carol the lights are put on.)

Vicar	After the seeking and the following
ALL	**Comes the answer and the truth**
Vicar	After the hustle and bustle of preparation
ALL	**Comes the calm and the stillness**
Vicar	After the waiting and the watching
ALL	**Comes the fulfilment of the promise**
Vicar	After the journey and the labour
ALL	**Comes the birth of hope and peace**

WAIT, WATCH, HOPE
Christingle 2008

CAST:

Michael	
Gabriel	
Elizabeth	
Mary	
Joseph	
Caspar	
Shepherds (3 or 4)	(Singing role)
Wise 'men'	Non speaking
Older angels: 5 In attendance on: Elizabeth Mary Joseph Caspar Shepherds	
Extra cherubs	

Notes

This is the longest of the plays. It is perhaps more suited to a carol service for a largely adult congregation, as there is not much action on stage and it assumes more knowledge on the part of the congregation. You could take the monologues out of it and use them by themselves as part of a more traditional carol service.

It is also the only play that gives Elizabeth a voice. She is a character who is too often neglected, but she is the first prophet of the New Testament, hailing Jesus as Messiah when he is still in the womb.

On the dais there should be 2 'director's chairs'. Behind them, facing the choir, two straw bales. There should be a number of placards on poles, reading: HOPE, WAIT, PREPARE, WATCH, SEEK, standing round the back of the front half of the dais.

There should be three stools or chairs positioned in front of the main aisle and the two side aisles between the banks of chairs

During the last verse of the carol, the older angels, with their cherub troops come down the aisle from the back and sit on the edges of the dais.

Elizabeth takes her seat on the left-hand stool

All readings are from the lectern on the left of the dais.

Throughout the scenes with the angels the younger angels should turn and pay attention to the archangels, reacting appropriately. Whenever the angels refer to God as HIM or HIS, everyone should look upwards briefly, and the word should be said as if it is in capitals.

(Left and right in these directions are as if you were standing by the door looking into the church.)

Suggested responses

Minister The evening is come and the night grows dark.

ALL **We wait and watch for the coming of our Lord.**

Minister One bright star shines above us.

ALL **We follow and seek for the coming of our Lord.**

Minister The angels sing their songs of joy.

ALL **And we bring our gifts and hearts to the manger.**

PROLOGUE: In the High Command of Heaven

(Michael takes his seat on one of the chairs. He is reading a newspaper.
Gabriel enters from the right and comes onto the dais.)

Michael Greetings, Gabriel.

Gabriel Greetings, Michael. Everything in hand?

Michael I think we're just about there. But this is a big one.
I don't think we've ever mounted an operation quite like this.

Gabriel *(With emphasis.)* In-car-na-tion. God becoming human. God living among mortals. God being born!
HE's never done this before.

Michael No. This is a once in an eternity experience.
It's important that nothing goes

123

	wrong. Do you hear that cherubs? Everything must go right, do you hear?
Cherubs	Yes, sir.
Michael	Have you got the list?
Gabriel	I have. Here it is. *(Produces a longish scroll.)* So many mortals to tell.
Michael	Be gentle with them, Gabriel. You can be a bit…startling at times. You're going to come as a shock you know.
Gabriel	Michael, you wound me. I'll be as soft as thistledown. As gentle as a dove.

(He goes to the left accompanied by the older angel with the placard reading HOPE and any cherubs who want to go with him/her. Wait by pillar on left.)

CAROL:	***On Christmas night all Christians sing***
READING:	***How Gabriel announced the birth of John the Baptist. Luke 1 vv 5 – 20***

SCENE 1:   **In Heaven**

(The older angel with the HOPE placard goes to stand beside Elizabeth. Gabriel returns to the dais, coming on from the left. Michael stands to greet him.)

124

Michael   Well, Gabriel? How did that go?

Gabriel   (*Sounding cross.*) Not quite what I'd bargained for, I must admit.

Michael   (*Indulgently.*) They're funny little things, mortals. Though I've got a soft spot for them.

Gabriel   The last thing I expected was that a priest wouldn't believe in me!

Michael   You'd think….being in the business, as it were…

Gabriel   Precisely! Instant recognition! And a good deal of respect.
Alas, no. Cheek, I call it. Standing there in the Holy of Holies, all dolled up in full regalia and daring to question to powers of HIM.

Michael   (*In an interrogatory tone.*) Gabriel, I'm starting to worry about this.

Gabriel   I confess it. I lost it with him.

Michael   (*In a tone that expects the worst.*) What did you do?

Gabriel   Shut his mouth for him. Oh, not permanently. It'll wear off once the baby's born. But it'll teach him a lesson he won't forget in a hurry.

Michael	(*Shaking his head.*) Gabriel. Gabriel. What are we going to do with you? That temper of yours!
Gabriel	I just couldn't help it. These humans! I always say, 'Don't be afraid' when I manifest myself. Might as well save my breath. How can they be so..so…. sceptical?
Michael	Gabriel, I'm ashamed of you. Don't you know they've got free will? They don't have to believe in you – marvellous as you are. It's their choice, not HIS, or yours. Now calm down and let's consider your next assignment.

(Both angels sit down.)

Elizabeth tells her story

(She stands to face outward.)

Elizabeth

When Zechariah came home from the Temple, struck dumb, I thought it was just one more of the curses that we had to bear.

It's a terrible thing, being barren, when all the friends you grew up with are having babies. You stay flat as a plank and there they are getting round and bonny and looking at you with pity.

And after a while they stop coming round to tell you the good news and inviting you to the parties. They think that something is wrong with you – that God is punishing you, for all your husband's a priest. And they don't want you tainting their happiness – or holding their babies. That hurt the worst.

And then, a husband stuck dumb!

He had to tell me what had happened, though. He couldn't hold it in. He acted it. He mimed it. I had to guess to help him along.

'A big bird?', 'An eagle?', - no – 'An angel?' – yes!

'Me? Getting fat?' – no, you can't mean.... . But he's rocking something in his arms! And patting my tummy! I could have cried – you can imagine.

From another man it would have been a cruel joke, but not from my Zechariah.

And then, over that long nine months, when I hardly dared to hope, he stayed with me at home – they wouldn't let him back in the temple. And so he taught me my letters – well, we couldn't spend the whole confinement miming at each other. So there on the kitchen table I learned to read.

Talking without speech. Reading each other's fingers and eyes. And the words forming on the tablet. As though we were children together again.

There are some blessings that are worth all the pain, all the long sad years. Blessings that are worth waiting for.

CAROL: *The Angel Gabriel to Mary came*
(During this carol Mary comes to sit on the stool in the centre. Gabriel goes to stand behind her together with the older angel with the placard that says WAIT.)

READING: **How Gabriel came to Mary**
Luke I vv 26 – 38

SCENE 2: **In Heaven**

Gabriel returns to the dais from the centre.
Michael   How did that one go?

Gabriel   Better, I suppose.
               Though it's jolly embarrassing when a
               teenage virgin asks you how she's

127

going to get pregnant! Is that any kind of question to ask an angel?

Michael   Did you tell her?

Gabriel   I didn't like to go into specifics.

Michael   It sounds as though she's a brave girl. She's going to need to be when you think what she's got in front of her.

Gabriel   Brave, yes. And gave a good reply, when I told her. A little more of what I'd call a proper respect for my rank.

Michael   So she said yes?

Gabriel   Of course she said yes. You don't expect her to say no, do you? When a full-grown archangel turns up in her kitchen. What girl's going to turn down that sort of honour?

Michael   She has a choice, Gabriel. Don't forget. All humans have a choice, even in the face of angelic manifestations. But it's not going to be easy for her. She's probably ruined her reputation, in human terms. You need to think carefully about how you're going to handle the next part of your mission.

(Both angels sit down.)

Mary tells her story
(Mary stands)

128

Mary

There's always people in our house. All over the place. There's never any time to yourself. No time to be alone.

You can't think. You can't pray. Always stuff to be done: floors to scrub, clothes to wash, water to fetch, chickens to feed, fire to tend, bread to knead.

'You wait till you're married,' says my mother. 'You won't know you're born, you'll have so much to do. There's plenty you need to learn, my girl.'

And then the angel came!

How did he manage to find the one time that it was quiet and I *was* alone? Mother out, the chores done, the bread baked, the kitchen warm and still.

Only an angel could have given me that moment. Only an angel.

And he *asked* me!

No-one *asks* me at home. It's do this and do that, and "Mary, Why haven't you done what *I* asked?"

He made me a promise. The baby will be the hope of the world. The one that we have always been waiting for.

So I said yes. …..I said yes. I *chose* yes.

But now it all changes. There's going to be a terrible row……and a lot of slapping, I should think. And I don't know what Joseph will say – or how I'm going to explain it to him.

(To herself, as a comforting thought.) The angel said not to be afraid.

CAROL: **When righteous Joseph wedded was***

* *This is a traditional carol but not very well known. The words fit well in the narrative though. For the shortened version we used see page 185.*

(During this carol Joseph comes to sit on his stool at the right hand side. Gabriel and the angel with the placard PREPARE go to stand beside him.)

READING: *How Gabriel came to Joseph in a dream*
Matthew 1 vv 18-24

SCENE 3: **In Heaven**

(Gabriel returns to the dais.)

Michael   Well, what happened this time?

Gabriel   This time, I did a dream appearance.
Well, he's called Joseph. I reckoned he might be like his famous namesake - and take dreams seriously.

Michael   A dream, eh? And less chance of any backchat, I suppose?

Gabriel   Trust you to think that.
He got the idea. I appealed to his better nature. He's a good, respectable man.

Michael   That doesn't always make for mercy – too concerned with keeping up appearances.

Gabriel   As I said – appeal to his *better* nature – the part that makes for kindness, for cherishing. For love without possessing.
So he chose to keep her.
He loves her you see. In spite of it all - the gossip, the snide remarks. All I had

130

Michael	to do was help him take that one, brave step.
Michael	And how did he feel about the baby – someone else's child?
Gabriel	He's always wanted a son. He'll treat him as his own. Adopt him. Give him his name. I did impress on him that it was rather an honour. You'll see. He'll be a good dad. How else does a baby learn about love?

(Both the angels sit down.)

Joseph tells his story
(He stands up.)
Joseph
Dreams are amazing things, aren't they?

With a name like Joseph, you get teased about it sometimes. 'Come on, my little dreamer,' my mum used to say.

I find you work things out in dreams.

Many's the time I've lain down puzzling over a design – how to cut the wood, how to angle the brace – and found the next morning it's all come clear, the wood easy to my hand, the angles all precise in my head.

You have to be patient, to be a carpenter.

Measure twice, cut once. That was dinned into me when I was a boy. You have to size up your wood, work with the grain. Sometimes the wood itself will show you how to work it. You find a better way of making something, better than you could have imagined when you first thought of it.

Like I said, dreams can show you how sometimes.

So, that dream.......with the angel.......
I know now what I'm going to do.
We're going to make a family, Mary and me – and the baby, when he comes. It isn't going to be what I planned. But we've got time to get used to the idea.

CAROL: ***Bethlehem of noblest cities***
(During the carol Caspar comes to stand at the back right and the angel with the placard SEEK together with the cherub who is to carry the star walks slowly off the dais and out to the Narthex where they collect the star.)

READING: ***How wise men came to seek out the Christ Child***
Matthew 2 vv 1-10

SCENE 4:   **In Heaven**

Gabriel   What's next, chief? Aren't there any other announcements to make?

Michael   There are. But I'm not sure that an angel messenger is right for the next one. It's a question of cultural references.

Gabriel   Uh?

Michael   We need to spread the word outside Israel, to all the people of the world. This isn't a private party. It's a cosmic event, once for all in space and time. The whole of humanity needs to hear about it.

Gabriel   How?

Michael   I've given this some thought. We need
to tell men of influence: scholars,
sages. People who will understand
what it means and can tell others.
Even pass it down the generations.
And we need a message that lots of
people can see and heed.

Gabriel   And your plan is?

Michael   A star.

Gabriel   A star?

Michael   A star. Not just any old star. An
amazing star, bigger than anything else
in the heavens. And they need it now,
so they get advance warning and can
start out in time to see the baby when
HE arrives.
In the right constellation it'll send such
a clear message that there'll be camels
whizzing all over the place.

*(As he says this the angel with the placard reading SEEK
comes in with a cherub with the star on a very long piece of
ribbon tied to her wrist. They come to stand at the back of
the dais.)*

Gabriel   Whizzing?

Michael   Trotting, galloping, galumphing –
whatever camels do when they're in a
hurry. You mark my words, there'll be
some very important travellers
seeking this baby.

133

(Angels sit down.)

Caspar tells his story
(He stands up.)
Caspar
I've waited all my life to see this – the birth of the prince of peace.

I've studied the ancient scriptures since I could first read. There were prophecies about the one who would come. One day, they said, one day, a child will be born, the salvation of humankind. One who will lead us back to our lost paradise. And the world will change forever. My fellow mages have studied the skies for years and recorded the heavens, looking always for this sign, a heavenly warning that the child was to be born. A triple conjunction of Jupiter and Saturn in Pisces – a sign of new birth in the land of the Hebrews.

And now it appears in the dawn sky.

I do not know where this will lead, but I am resolved to follow it.

The older ones call me a foolish youth.

Some say I am a fool, for all my learning – to go off, heaven knows where, in search of a …what? My mother says that I am neglecting my responsibilities – that I should choose to stay at home and look after her instead. What do I think I will find, she says.

A child? A king? A dream?

But what's my life worth if I always stay in the same place, safe. Unless we seek, unless we question, - isn't it that that makes us human?

Well, here we go, not knowing what we seek, but being sure that we will know when we have found it.

(The other wise men, who have been sitting to the side join him and they process round the dais and round to the back of the choir seats. The star angel leads them.)

134

(During the carol, Mary and Joseph get up from their stools and join hands. They walk round the dais and sit on the straw bales.

Elizabeth goes to sit back down in the congregation.

Their respective angels should move the stools and then follow to the manger where they form a semi circle behind the holy family

The shepherds should group themselves round the font, seated on the ground.)

READING: ***How the shepherds heard the good news***
Luke 2 vv 1-15

SCENE 5: **In Heaven**

Michael   Last announcement, Gabriel. Last glorious announcement!

Gabriel   HE's there, isn't HE? HE's really done it!

Michael   HE's there. Mother and baby both doing well, as they say down there.

Gabriel   It isn't quite as I'd expected – stable and manger. I thought that it might be more.. well… tidy, clean, comfortable. More fitting for HIS status, if you get my drift.

Michael   It isn't a royal progress, Gabriel. This is ordinary life, with ordinary people – the way life is for most of them, not the rich and favoured.

Gabriel   What's the point of being all-powerful then?

Michael   You've been mixing with mortals just a little bit too much, Gabriel. You've started to think about power the way that they do – all based on money and strength and fear. You know better than that.

Heaven's only power, HIS only power, lies in Love. To the world that's weakness, foolishness. But it's the only way that gives a choice, Gabriel, the only way that lets humans have their marvellous life, full of choices and chances.

Now off you go to those poor outcast shepherds and catch them up in the joy of the moment.

Gabriel   This time, I am taking the whole of the heavenly host. We're going to sing the sheepskins off them!

Michael   Don't scare them too much.

Gabriel   Come on chaps!

(All the angels get to their feet and follow Gabriel about halfway down the aisle.
The shepherds get to their feet in alarm.
They sing, to the tune People look East, or England's Lane:)

Angels   Sing, O sing, this blessed morn,
(with the   unto us a child is born,
women   unto us a son is given,
from the   God himself comes down from heaven.
choir)   Sing, O sing, this blessed morn,

Jesus Christ today is born.

Shepherds (with men from the choir)	God of God and Light of Light, comes with mercies infinite, joining in a wondrous plan heaven to earth and God to man.
All	**Sing, O sing, this blessed morn, Jesus Christ today is born.**
All	**God comes down that we may rise, lifted by him to the skies; Christ is Son of Man that we sons of God in him may be. Sing, O sing, this blessed morn, Jesus Christ today is born.***

CHRISTINGLE PROCESSION FOLLOWS:
The whole congregation are invited to bring their gifts to the manger, see the real baby and collect a Christingle. The candles are lit and the children sing Away in a Manger. Prayers for the work of the Children's Society are said, followed by the Lord's Prayer.

EPILOGUE

(The angels are back on the dais. Michael is reading his paper.
Gabriel rushes in and skids to a halt.)

Gabriel   Well, that was a close shave!

Michael   (Startled.) What happened?

---

* *This carol is by Christopher Wordsworth, 1862.*

Gabriel   Herod! What possessed our so-called wise men!? Blundering into the palace asking for the heir presumptive! Don't they know Herod's reputation? He's already murdered two of his sons in case they try to seize the throne.

Michael   What did he do?

Gabriel   Sent a troop of soldiers to kill the baby – to kill HIM!
But they're safe away. I warned Joseph in another dream. He and Mary took to the hills – the shepherds will guide them safely on their way. And I made sure, - more dreams - that the wise men are off home by another route.

Michael   Good work and quick thinking, Gabriel.

Gabriel   In the nick of time, Michael. Goodness, it's a risky business, this human existence. All those choices and chances. How do they cope, humans, I mean. How do they do it? Live their lives in all that uncertainty and danger?

Michael   That's what makes it life, Gabriel. All those choices and chances, risks and dangers. Because it's full of hope and love as well, and fun and beauty and excitement.
(Goes to the edge of the dais, with his arm round Gabriel's shoulders and looks out over the congregation and into the distance.)

Look at them all Gabriel. Aren't they amazing. Watching and waiting, hoping and seeking. All part of HIS marvellous creation. All created by HIS love. And HE's gone to be with them, to share it all, to be part of it too. Somewhere out there Gabriel. Somewhere out there.

CAROL:	***It came upon the midnight clear,***
	(During this carol the angels all process off the dais down the aisle and into the Narthex. Gabriel and Michael bring up the rear.)

BLESSING

THE WORD
THE CHOICE
THE BIRTH
Christingle 2011

CAST

The Plain People:	*Between 3 and 5 characters who change their costumes and voices for each of the scenes.*
Mary	
Gabriel	*Plus cherubs who may accompany him in the shepherds' scene*
Joseph	
3 shepherds	
Star	
3 Wise Men: Caspar, Melchior, Balthazar	
2 pages *(or more)*	*You may omit them*

Notes

The Plain People are like a Greek chorus to the drama. The dialogue needs dividing up between them, depending on how many you have. They form by turn:

women at the town pump*: costumes: shawls and aprons, brooms and buckets;*

men of the town*: bowlers/trilbies, painters' overalls, toolbox, spade/other working implements, newspapers;*

other shepherds*: old Barbour jackets, flat caps, crooks/walking sticks;*

court advisers*: turbans, fezes, other 'exotic' headgear, robes, jewels.*

Staging:

Dais empty apart from chair and low bed (at start) to left hand side.

Chancel screened off in some way, to form the stable

Scripture: *I used J B Phillips' The Gospels in Modern English* [*] *for the scripture passages in this service. I would recommend its crisp clarity. The Reader is acting a little more like a narrator to the play.*

SERVICE

Choir sing from the balcony – the first two verses and choruses of Christ be our Light (see Common Ground* for words and music)

Bidding:

  Minister

  On this Christmas Eve, we welcome you all to our Christingle Service.

  We will hear again how the angels brought good news

---

[*] *Pub. Geoffrey Bles, London, 1957*
[*] *Pub. Saint Andrew Press, Edinburgh, 2003*

to humans and asked them to take part in God's great
work of incarnation, as God himself became human
and shared with us the risks, the fears, the hopes, the
loves of our lives.
And we will hear how Mary and Joseph, the shepherds
and the wise men responded to the heavenly call and
helped bring the Word to birth.
In our own lives, we pray that the Good News of
God's Word may become part of us, so that we too
may bring the Word to birth, showing love and
compassion to everyone our lives touch.
And so, remembering how Jesus taught us to pray to
God as his father and our father we say together the
prayer he taught us:

Lord's Prayer

Carol: *In the bleak midwinter*

*(During carol Mary takes her place on the chair. She is sewing
something and giving it all her attention.*
*The Plain People also take their place sitting to the right of the
dais. They are dressed as the women of the town.)*

Reader: *(From lectern.)*
              **Luke 1 vv 26 and 27 (Omit "In the
              sixth month")**

*(Gabriel comes running down the aisle and jumps onto the
dais. Mary jumps up and gives a small shriek as though she
has pricked her finger.)*

Gabriel   Mary! Greetings, beloved of God!

Mary   Who are you?
              What do you want?
              How did you get in?

Gabriel   The Lord be with you, Mary. Fear not.
                I am Gabriel, one of the angels who
                attend before the most High God and
                do his bidding.
                *(Takes her hand and sits her back down on
                the chair. Kneels before her.)*
                Mary, God loves you dearly and he
                wants you to be the mother of his son,
                the Messiah, the one foretold by the
                prophets. The saviour of his people.

Mary   A baby?

Gabriel   Yes – God's son. You will call him Jesus.

Mary   Me? Have a baby?
                How can I? I'm not married.

Gabriel   God can do anything, Mary, by his Holy
                Spirit.

Mary   *(With a wail of panic.)*
                But what will people say?

(Mary and Gabriel freeze. The Plain People get up, and say:)

Plain people

-       No better than she ought to be, I've always
        said.

-       Her poor mother, having to live with the
        shame.

-       Her daft father more like. Should have given
        her a good hiding.

-       Spare the rod and spoil the child, that what I
        always say.

- She always was a flighty one.
- Head in the clouds.
- Too much reading – no good ever comes of it.
- Nobody will marry her now, least of all Joseph.
- Nobody *respectable*.
- They should turn her out on the street.
- Good riddance too.
- They'd have stoned her in the old days.
- Quite right too. Shocking I call it.
- *(Shaking head.)* Ruined…..ruined.
- *(Said with relish.)* Her reputation will never recover now.

Choir or solo *(Sing from balcony – to the tune of the chorus of Christ be our light.)*
Choose, Mary, choose
Choose for us now,
Choose for the future.
Choose, Mary, choose.
Give God your heart,
  Free us today
(During this the Plain People sit down.
At the end Mary and Gabriel unfreeze, and she stands up and takes his hands.)

Mary   Angel, I choose yes. I belong to the Lord and will serve him body and soul in whatever he wishes.

(Gabriel embraces her and leads her off the dais as the Carol starts.
During the carol a bed is placed where the chair was, and the People change into their townsmen's costumes.)

CAROL: *The angel Gabriel from heaven came*

Reader   *(From lectern.)*
Matthew 1, vv 18 and 19, then continue with:
He was thinking this over one night when he went to bed.

(Joseph comes onto the stage, gets into the bed and pulls the covers over himself.
Gabriel comes in from the side, this time tiptoeing very carefully, whispering Shhh to the congregation if they laugh!
He stands by Joseph's head and calls to him.)

Gabriel   Joseph! Joseph. Listen to what I have to say to you.

Joseph   *(In his sleep.)*
Yes. Yes.

Gabriel   I am Gabriel, one of the angels who attend before the most High God and do his bidding.
He sends you a message.

Joseph   *(Mumbles.)*

Gabriel   You must not cast Mary aside. She is telling the truth. She is bearing God's own son. She has not been unfaithful to you.
Marry her and bring up the baby.
Call him Jesus. He will save his people.

146

He is the promised Messiah.

Joseph *(In his sleep.)* But the neighbours…..

(The Plain People get up, and say:)
Plain People

- You're a fool to yourself, man.

- You don't want a cuckoo in the nest.

- You wouldn't catch me bringing up another man's child.

- She'll play you false.

- You'll never be able to trust her.

- You're besotted, man!

- She needs showing what's what!

- If it was me, I'd give her a good walloping.

- Mind you, I blame her parents.

- Far too soft, the pair of them.

- You're never going to pay a bride price after this.

- Soiled goods, that's what she is.

- You could do better, man. A fine respectable citizen like you.

- With your own business and all.

- Someone's got to take a stand, you know.

- In the old days they'd have stoned her.

- Quite right too. What's the world coming to?

Choir or *(Sing from balcony – to the tune of the chorus*
solo *of Christ be our light.)*
Choose, Joseph, choose.
Choose for us now,
Choose for the future.
Choose, Joseph, choose.
Give God your heart,
Free us today

(During this the Plain People sit down, and Gabriel goes off the dais to side. Joseph wakes up and collects the bed and goes off as the reading continues.)

Reader So Joseph woke from sleep and carried out the instructions of the angel of the Lord. He married Mary and took care of her.

Carol: *When our God came to earth*

(During the carol the Plain People change into shepherds' clothes.
Mary and Joseph need to get to the back of the church so that they can come down the nave during the next reading.)

Reader *(From lectern.)*
Luke 2 vv 1- 7

(The three Shepherds have followed Mary and Joseph and come down the aisle to sit on the floor in front of the dais.)

Reader **Luke 2, v 8**

(Gabriel leaps onto the dais from the back, ideally holding a big bright torch which he shines on the shepherds, who cower. If there are cherubs, they accompany him with torches.)

Gabriel   Fear not!
I am bringing you good news of a great joy
– a joy for all the people of the world.
Today, in David's town of Bethlehem, a
baby has been born, who will be your
Saviour, the Messiah, the Lord!
Go and see him!
This is how you will know him.
You will find him wrapped in swaddling
bands and lying in a manger.

Choir   *(Sing Gloria – Taizé chant or anything else that
seems suitable.)*

*(Gabriel goes off. The Plain People get up and stand up on
the dais looking at the shepherds. They speak in slow
Yorkshire voices (or your local accent):)*

Plain People

-              A likely tale.

-              A Messiah in a manger!

-              Fat lot of good a babby's going to do.

-              Womanish, I call it, Fussing over a babby.

-              Who's to say it'll live. Plenty die that young.

-              You wouldn't catch me going all the way
down there.

-              Who was that creature anyway?

-              A Saviour in a stable! Not bloomin' likely!

-              You must be daft.

-              You'll not be leaving the sheep.

-              No, you'll not be leaving the sheep.

- Not on a night like this.

- Not with the wolves around.

- If t'mester finds you've left them! Well!

- I wouldn't want to be in thy shoes.

- You'll not have shoes if t'mester finds out

- Best do nowt.

- Best bide here.

- You can't get done for that.

- Don't be fools, lads. Stay put.

Choir or solo *(Sing from balcony – to the tune of the chorus of Christ be our light.)*
Choose, Shepherds, choose.
Choose for us now,
Follow the angel.
Choose, Shepherds, choose.
Seek out the child,
Find him today

(During this the Plain People sit down, and the Shepherds stand up.)

S1 You heard what he said. The Messiah! In our lifetime!

S2 I'm going. Try to stop me!

S3 It's not every day you see an angel. It was an angel wasn't it?

S1 A whole host of them.

S2 They'll take care of the sheep.

S3   The Lord's our shepherd – he'll know what
                to do.

(They pick up their stuff and make their way round the dais.)

Reader   *(From lectern.)*
                Luke 2, vv 16 - 20

CAROL: *Brightest and best of the sons of the morning*

(During the carol the Plain People change into their court costumes The wise men assemble at about the font at the back. The star- a helium balloon tied to the wrist of a child – comes onto the dais, and stands a little in front of and to the side of the Reader.)

Reader   Jesus was born in Bethlehem, in Judea,
                in the days when Herod was king of the
                province. Wise men in the east saw his
                star in the sky.

Caspar   Look, my brothers. There is the star
                that I told you of. Every night it grows
                brighter.

Melchior   I have never seen a star so bright and
                beautiful.

Balthazar   I have looked up the conjunction. It
                certainly means that a new king has
                been born.

Caspar   Yes, but no ordinary king. The records
                say a prince of peace.

Melchior A servant king – how is one to explain the paradox?

Balthazar It seems to me that I must go. I must travel to see this new king.

Caspar And I too. We will never see his like again.

Melchior And take the finest tribute that we can bring.

Balthazar Yes, gold and precious spices and perfumes.

Caspar The richest treasures of our kingdoms.

Page 1 Sir, may we come?

Page 2 May we come too and see the child?

(The Plain People get up and form a cordon across the stage with their arms folded. Smooth posh snooty voices.)
Plain People

- My Lords, be guided by me. Abandon this quest.

- It can only lead to disappointment.

- The people of those parts are very backward.

- The stars can be so misleading.

- Oracles are notoriously ambiguous.

- The kingdom really cannot manage if you abscond.

-	Your presence is needed here.
-	Where your duty lies.
-	Your people need you.
-	We can ill afford such precious gifts.
-	The roads are very bad at this time of year.
-	Think about the bandits on the way, the robbers….
-	The inconvenience….
-	No hot baths for weeks…
-	Dreadful meals in primitive inns….
-	Fleas…bedbugs…..insanitary privies…
-	Is your journey really necessary?
-	Couldn't a messenger go instead?
-	An envoy perhaps?
-	An emissary?
Choir or solo	*(Sing from balcony – to the tune of the chorus of Christ be our light.)* Choose, wise men, choose Choose for us now, Follow the starlight. Choose, wise men, choose. Seek out the child, For the whole world.

(During the singing the Plain People remain in their line.)

Caspar	Gentlemen, we thank you for your counsel, but there are some things that go beyond and above reason and

prudence and we are resolved on this
journey.
(The Plain People do not move.)
We are, as I say, resolved.

Pages   And so are we!

*(The wise men move forward and the Plain People go off to
the right shaking their heads and sit down in their usual
place.)*

Reader   *(From lectern.)*
               Matthew 2 vv 1 – 2, 7 – 11

*(During the reading the wise men stay in the aisle until 'And
now the star..'' and then they follow it around the dais and
behind the screen.)*

**The congregation is then invited to come to the
stable to see the baby, make an offering and
collect a Christingle. The candles are then lit.
Prayers are said.
The lights are put out and the children sing Away
in a Manger.
The candles are blown out and there are final
prayers, a blessing and a final carol.**

BABOUSHKA
Christingle 2012

CAST	
Beth	*A widowed, nosy woman*
Keziah	*Her younger neighbour*
Keziah's children	*3-4 of them*
Mary	
Joseph	
3 shepherds	
Cherubs	*These are optional, if you have enough small children who would like to take part*
3 kings	

Notes:

This play is based on the Russian legend of Baboushka, who is the Russian children's Father Christmas, bringing them presents and leaving them in their shoes. I have taken some liberties with the traditional tale.

We dressed Beth and Keziah in generic peasant women costumes: big skirts, aprons, shawls, and the children and shepherds in similar attire.

This is another play with an after piece, which takes place after the Christingle giving and the visit to the stable. It was very moving when Beth came back in tears and the children liked her giving out sweets at the end.

When we staged this we took the congregation round to the corridor and rooms at the back of the church to find the stable and one of the church members made a fine set of signposts and hotel signs, with FULL UP, to decorate the route.

Minister:

On this Christmas Eve, we welcome you all to our Christingle Service.

Tonight we hear again the story of the birth of Jesus, the Prince of Peace, God born amongst us to share our human life. And we will hear how people responded to this news, and went to see the new-born child.

And as we remember The Children's Society and bring our gifts for its work we remember that every child is a holy child, each one of us, made in God's image.

As we listen, and sing, and come to the manger, we ask that in our hearts we will find that childlike trust and wonder that opens for us the Kingdom of Heaven.

And so, as God's children, we say together the prayer that Jesus taught us:

Our Father....

CAROL: On Christmas night all Christians sing

READING: Mary and Joseph come to Bethlehem. *Luke 2 vv 1- 7*

SCENE 1: A hamlet about a mile from Bethlehem

(The dais is cleared of everything apart from two wooden kitchen chairs.

Keziah, a younger woman, comes in from the left with a basket. She is a busy mother and has just got her children to bed. She sits down on the left hand chair and starts to do some sort of domestic task - shelling peas, sorting clothes or mending, or knitting.

Beth comes in from the right. She is older than Keziah, a widow whose only child died in infancy. She fills her days with obsessive housework and interfering in other people's lives. She is wearing a voluminous apron and sweeping as she goes (ideally with an old fashioned straw or besom broom). She reaches the chair nearest her and sits down, huffing and puffing a bit.)

Keziah   Evening, Beth. Tasks all done then?

Beth   Evening Keziah. Just about, I'd say. There's that much to do. The dust gets everywhere, don't it. Whoever said a woman's work was never done had it just about right, I reckon. Still, it's good to sit down in the evening and watch the world go by, just for a bit.

Keziah   There's been that many people going past today. All on their way to Bethlehem for the census. The place'll be bursting.

Beth   Typical foreign notion, counting people. No sense in it, I say. Folk should stay put. What do they want to go travelling for? As if there isn't enough to do at home. You look as if you haven't finished your chores either.

Keziah   (*A little defensively. She knows she's being got at for being feckless.*)
Oh I like to keep these little jobs for a sit down in the evening.

Beth   Well, I'll not interfere in your business.
(*Sits back in her chair.*)
Here's some more people coming.

(*Mary and Joseph start to make their way down the aisle. They are both tired and Mary is finding it hard to walk.*)

Beth   Well, would you look at that! What's she doing on the road? She's in no fit state to travel.

Keziah   I should think she's due any day now.

Beth   (*Sourly.*) Well, you should know. You've had plenty of practice.
Shameless, I call it. She should be at home, not flaunting herself. There are no standards any more.
(*She folds her arms firmly across her chest.*)

(*By this time Joseph and Mary have got nearly to the dais.*)

Joseph   Look, Mary. Houses. Maybe we're nearly there. I'll ask the women.

Mary   Joseph. I think I'd better. They might not like

being spoken to by a strange man. *(Moves towards the women.)*
Excuse me. If you please, can you tell me how far Bethlehem is from here?

Keziah   *(Standing up and coming to the edge of the dais.)* Well, yes, of course. It's only about a mile along this road. You should be there before it gets dark.

Beth   *(Standing up too and coming to stand by Keziah, hands on hips and rather aggressive.)* And what do you think you're doing, travelling in your state. Is that your husband? What's he thinking of making you travel in your condition?

Mary   *(Falling straight into the trap.)* He's my fiancé … and we had to come because of the decree.

Beth   *(Affronted.)* Not even married. Shameless. You, my girl, ought to be at home with your mother, not gallivanting to please Rome.

(Mary retreats into Joseph's arms.)

Keziah   Oh Beth, she's only young, give over. She needs to rest.

Beth   It's never too early to learn the proper way of going about things.
And she's not staying here. We're respectable folks here. I'm not having a baggage like that and her fancy man – yes,

young man, I do mean you – in my nice clean house, and neither are you, Keziah. *Your reputation will go down like a stone.*

Joseph   Mary, come away. Don't listen to them. They have no idea what they are talking about. You leave her alone, do you hear!

Beth   *(Picking up the broom.)* Be off the pair of you and good riddance. We don't want your sort round here.

(She waves the broom to shoo them away and they go off to the back of the chancel. Both women sit back down.)

Keziah   *(Timidly.)* You were a bit harsh, Beth. They didn't mean any harm.

Beth   That's what you think. There's all sorts out there. Thieves and tricksters. Let alone foolish girls who've got themselves in the family way without being wed. Once a woman's reputation's gone, she's nothing. You can't be too careful these days. Mark my words.

(During the following carol the women leave the stage.)

CAROL: *See him lying on a bed of straw*

READING: **How the Shepherds heard the good news**
Luke 2, vv 8 - 17

SCENE 2: A hamlet about a mile from Bethlehem

(As before, the two women come onto the stage. Beth first this time, and sits down with the air of one who has done a tiring day's work. Keziah follows, a bit hot and bothered.)

Keziah   Evening, Beth.

Beth   Evening, Keziah. You're a bit late tonight. Children playing up, are they?

Keziah   I though I'd never get them to go to bed. They're that restless, and the animals are acting strange too. You'd think there was a thunderstorm brewing, or an earthquake.

Beth   You shouldn't say such things. Heaven preserve us.
But I know what you mean. Then hens wouldn't get in the hen house like they usually do. I had to chase them in with my broom.

Keziah   Still, it's nice and peaceful now.

(Both women stretch on their chairs comfortably and sit companionably, but the quiet is broken with a riotous noise from the back as the shepherds come through the doors.)

Beth   You spoke too soon. What on earth is that?

(Both women stand up and shade their eyes to look down the aisle. The shepherds appear a little bit tipsy. They are doing a

sort of jig as they go. They might embrace the members of the congregation who are sitting at the edge of the aisle. They are singing in a rather raucous way, the chorus from 'Angels from the realms of glory'': Come and worship… *If there are plenty of cherubs some of them can be with the shepherds holding their hands as though they are leading them along. Use the shaded lines, if you have them.)*

Beth   Drunken louts. Shepherds by the look of them. Filthy dirty and no morals – no manners either. Up on those hills with no-one to keep them decent.
(Raises voice.) What do you think that you're doing, cavorting like this, disturbing the peace. Be off with you. We're decent, God-fearing folk here.

Shep 1   Peace? Missis?
You don't know anything about it.

Shep 2   We've seen a heavenly messenger.

Shep 3   Aye, an angel. Told us all about peace he did.

Shep 1   Peace on earth and good will to everybody.

Cherubs   *(Loudly.)* Peace on earth and good will to everybody!

Keziah   Sssh. You'll wake my children. I've only just got them to bed
What are you talking about?

(At this point, Keziah's children, who have been at the side of the dais in the front row, do start to wake up and creep up behind her chair very quietly.)

Shep 2   Beg pardon, Missis. But this news is too
good.
We can't be quiet.
He's come, the Messiah's come!

Beth   What nonsense is this?

Shep 3   'S'not nonsense, Missis. We've seen an
angel. We've been sent to find the baby.

Shep 1   Wrapped up in a manger in Bethlehem.

Shep 2   So we come as quick as we could.

Beth   What rubbish! Why would the Messiah of
all people be found in a stable? A likely
tale.

Shep 3   There were hundreds of angels. *(Gestures
to the cherubs)* Look.

Beth   Angels – *(sniff)* – Urchins more like. They
should be tucked up in bed fast asleep

Shep 1   Sky was full of them.
We've got to go there.

Shep 2   Come with us, ladies. It's what the whole
world's been waiting for. You can't miss it.

163

Keziah's children	Oh mother, please can we go!
Keziah	What are you doing out of bed?
Children	Oh mother, please.
Shep 1	Oh go on, Missis. To think that we should live to see it.
Shep 2	You can't miss it.
Beth	Keziah, I'm surprised at you. If they were my children, I'd give them what for.
Keziah	(*Suddenly bolder, taking off her apron.*) But they're not yours, they're mine, and you can keep your sour old tongue to yourself. He's right. The Messiah, Beth. Of course we're all going. So what if he's in a stable. Don't they say that ox and ass know their own master? Quick children, get your things.

(*They scurry to the seats and pull on scarves and shawls, and the whole group start singing again and go off through the chancel and out the back door by the organ.*
Shepherd 1 offers Beth his arm, but she threatens him with her broom and sits down with her arms folded firmly across her chest.
She leaves the dais during the next carol.)

CAROL: *Angels from the realms of glory*

SCENE 3: A hamlet about a mile from Bethlehem

(As before, Beth comes out to sit down outside her house. She starts this in the last verse of the carol and gives the dais a punitive sweeping. A small angel with a star comes down the aisle as the carol ends and goes past her to the back of the chancel where s/he pauses. Beth pays it no attention, and carries on with her knitting/darning/ patching.
She does however, look up at the jingling of bells from the back as the Kings (plus retinue) enter and proceed slowly down the nave.
She stands up and shields her eyes to look down the road.)

Beth   Time was, this was a respectable neighbourhood: no foreigners and nothing unexpected happening. I don't know what the world's coming to.
Mind you, this lot look a bit of quality. Fancy robes, jewels. Hmmm. The bettermost sort, I'd say.

(She smooths her headscarf and takes her apron off.
The group get to the dais and they all bow to her, saying, one after the other:)

Kings   Good evening.
                    Good evening.
                          Good evening.

Beth   *(Making rather a flustered curtsey.)* Good evening, your, your *(Searches for the right* *word.)*... worships.

King 1   Dear madam, can you direct us to Bethlehem?

Beth   *(Squeakily.)* Madam!

King 2   They told us at King Herod's palace that this was the road that we should take.

Beth   Palace!

King 3   We are seeking the new born Prince of Peace.

Beth   Prince of Peace!

King 1   *(Slightly impatiently.)* Madam. Is this the Bethlehem road?

Beth   *(Bobbing another curtsey, and getting a grip on herself.)* Oh yes, Sirs. Yes it is. You just keep straight on. It's only another mile.

King 2   Madam, we thank you.

(They start to turn. Beth summons a bit of courage and puts on a posher voice.)

Beth   But won't you stop – remain - a while? It would be an honour to have you in my house. You look as if you've come a long way.

King 3   Madam, we study the heavens, we have, as you say, travelled many miles, led by that star, to seek your prince of peace – Messiah, I believe you say - your Christ Child.

King I   But we cannot stay, though we thank you for your kindness.

King 2   We must find this child and lay our treasures at his feet.

Beth   Treasures!

King 3   Come with us, dear lady. Come and see this wonder.

Beth   Me! With you!

King I   We will escort you safely to pay your homage too.

Beth   It's not very proper, running off with a party of gentlemen – even if you are – well, that is to say – I can see you're very grand, and very learned…

King 2   This is not a night for respectable scruples, Madam. This is God's change for the whole world. How can you not be there? Even King Herod is coming to worship him.

Beth   King Herod! *(Bobs another curtsey.)* Well, I thank you kindly. I will come.

But, but, I'll not hold you up.
I'll just tidy the house and find a present
for the baby and lock things up and I'll
follow you on. I know the way.

(The kings and their party all bow. Beth curtsies again.)

King I   Madam, farewell. We will meet you again
in Bethlehem.

*(The kings process off down the chancel and the star goes
before them through the back door.*
*Beth, left behind, goes into a tizzy. She ties he apron back
on.)*

Beth   I'll just sweep up and scrub the table and
bank the fire down and find a basket of
things for the baby. It wouldn't do to turn
up empty handed. What sort of a
welcome would that be? There's my
Simon's baby things he never lived to play
with, but goodness, they'll need a wash
after all these years.....
(And she goes off to her side.)

CAROL: *As with gladness men of old*

Invitation to all to come to the stable

*(Once everyone is back in their seats and as the Christingles
are being lit Beth appears on the dais again. She may have to
wait for quiet. Strategic shushing may need to take place.)*

Beth   Right, that's everything done and tidy and
safe. I'll be on my way to see the Christ child
then.

I've got a lovely basket of things for him.
To think, that I should live to see this day!
(And she goes off to the back and through the back door.)

Prayer over the Christingles
Away in a Manger
Christingle prayer
Prayer for the new children

(Beth comes back in from the left side and up to the dais. She is very upset.)

Beth   Oh. Oh. Oh. When I got there, they said that he'd gone. The baby and his father and mother. He *was* there. He *was* in the stable just like the angels said – and I was too late.

Oh, I've been a foolish old woman. How will I ever find him now?

How will I even show him my love?

…..

Well, I'm not giving up. I shall walk the world until I find him.

How will I know him?

Any child might be the one…

(Pause as she works it out.)

Every child will be the Christ Child to me. I'll not miss my chance the second time.

Every child shall have a present from my basket.

For every child is a holy child.

(And she marches off down the aisle and takes her stand by the door with her basket of sweets for the children as they go out.)

Final Carol
Blessing

THE CRIB SET
Christingle 2013

CAST:	
Angel	
Joseph	
Mary	
Shepherds	*Two speakers*
Wise men	*Only Balthazar speaks*
Cherubs,	*If you have available small children*
2 women, Doris and Gladys,	*Whose voices we hear in the first scene – this could be recorded and played over the sound system*

Notes

The idea for this year's play came to me as I was unpacking an old set of crib figures that we had found when clearing out some cupboards in the church. They needed a good deal of dusting and a bit of repair. Like many such figures though, they seemed to have a dignity and life of their own.

I wrote it so that only a few of the figures have speaking parts; this was because of the constraints of our microphone system, which means that only a limited number of people can have the lapel mikes. If the sound system is better the parts among the wise men and shepherds could be spread out a little more.

Costumes should be of the rather traditional crib figure type. The Angel needs a set of feathery angel wings.

When the scenes finish the crib figures need to freeze, ideally in their crib poses. You can have a nice bit of business if your actors need to wear spectacles, with them whipping them off each time they freeze.

For the set you need what appears to be a very large cardboard box. We constructed ours with a light wooden frame to which we fastened (with a staple gun) sheets of cardboard from appliance boxes – it was amazing how many boxes the congregation were able to supply. We marked it in large painted letters: 'CRIB FIGURES' and 'FRAGILE'. There was a separate smaller box for the cherubs.

The service starts in darkness and the choir sing.
Words of welcome are spoken by the Minister
The Lord's Prayer
SCENE 1:

(Recorded voices, or miked voices from the balcony.)

Gladys   Well, that's it, Doris. I've found the Advent wreath.

Doris   And I've found the candles.

172

Gladys   Nearly ready for Christmas then. Bob's got all the lights sorted and untangled.

Doris   And I've put the boxes of decorations out for the tree.

Gladys   And here are the crib figures, all in their box. [Oh, and the box of cherubs.]* Look, just as they were when we put them away.

Doris   Go on with you. You'd think, to hear you talk, that they have lives of their own.

Gladys   Well, I do sometimes wonder what they get up to when we're gone. I can't help it, they look so lifelike sometimes when you come in and the church is all empty and there they are in the stable.

Doris   What have you got there? Or *who*, should I say?

Gladys   It's a new angel. D'you remember? The old one got broken when we were putting them away last year. Alice smashed him on the end of the table – by accident, I mean. So I ordered a new one from Kevin Mayhew. I'll just pop him in.
(Rustle.) There you go, be good.

Doris   The others'll have to teach him what to do.

---

* *Shaded words in square brackets can be used if you have some small people to play cherubs*

Gladys   Listen to you now. They'll think we're going daft.
              How about a cup of coffee before we lock up…
              (Voices fade away with footsteps.)

CAROL: Long ago, prophets knew

SCENE 2:

(The set consists of what appears to be a very large cardboard box, about 8' square and 3' high. This takes up most of the dais. The Angel is standing very stiffly beside the box. Mary and Joseph are outside the box, but wrapped in newspaper and lying down. The rest of the figures are in the box, with newspaper wrappings.)

Joseph   *(Standing up and untangling himself. He is an older, fatherly figure.)* Hey, come on team. Move on, move up! Rise and shine. It's okay. The coast's clear. It's time to wake up again for Christmas.

(The others start to stir, unpeeling paper wrappings as they do so, but only Shepherd 1 and Balthazar stand up, in the box, at this stage.)

Shepherd 1 By 'eck, I'm stiff. I've been jammed in the corner all year with Balthazar's slippers up my nose. Stilton ain't in it.

Balthazar   *(Who I imagine sounds a little like Brian Sewell. Perhaps a little camp. Loftily.)* You can talk! I've had the camel in intimate proximity for eleven months!

Joseph   *(Helping Mary up.)* Hey, Mother Mary. Are you all right? Not too squashed, I hope?

Mary   No. Thank you Joseph. I'm fine. Just a little stiff, that's all. Is it really nearly a year since they put us away?
(Sees the angel.) Oh! Who are you?

Joseph   *(When the angel doesn't immediately respond.)* He'll be the new Angel, Mother Mary. You remember. Last year Old Gabriel never came back to the box.

(There is a pause where all the figures reverently bow their heads in respect.)

Angel   *(Sounding a bit uneasy)* They just put me in here. Just now. I don't know what's happening or how I got here. Who are you all?

Joseph   Easy lad. There's nothing to be alarmed at. Bless me, what do they teach them at the manufacturers nowadays?

Shepherd 1   We're the crib figures. We help make Christmas come alive for the humans.

Balthazar   They put us in the stable.

Mary   And then everybody knows it's Christmas.

Angel   What's Christmas?

(Shocked reactions from all the other figures!)

Joseph   Shocking ignorance!

Balthazar It's when God's son, when God, came to be with humans, to be like them.

Mary   He was my baby, born in a stable.

Shepherd 1 And the angels came and told us. That's you.

Angel   Me!

Joseph   Calm down, lad. We'll soon break you in – so to speak. You're an Angel.

Angel   I am!?

Joseph   The wings are a dead giveaway.
               You've got a very important part in the story.

Angel   I do!?

Joseph   You're God's messenger. That's what angel means.

Angel   I am!?

Joseph   You are, lad. So calm down and listen carefully. Soon the humans will be taking us all out of the box and putting us in the stable in the Prayer Corner* for Christmas. One by one, we help them tell the

_____

* *If you don't have a Prayer Corner, adapt this.*

176

Christmas story.
They'll take Mary first.

Angel   Why?

Mary   Because that's how the story starts. The angel – that's you – came to tell me that I was going to have a baby, even though, at that time, I wasn't married.

Angel   Hang on, even I know that's not supposed to happen.

Mary   *(Hastily.)* But I was engaged though.

Angel   Congratulations. Who's the lucky fellow?

Joseph   That would be me, lad. I'm Joseph.

Angel   So, I tell Mary she's having your baby....Hasn't she guessed already?

Joseph   It's not that simple, lad. This is God's baby. This is God, in human form, come to share an earthly life. That's what makes it so special for humans. It's what makes them come alive too, you might say.

Mary   Quick, someone's coming. They'll be practising the readings

Angel   But...

Joseph   Freeze, lad. And pin your ears back.

(All the characters freeze in their positions.)

SCENE 3

(During the carol Mary goes off behind the chancel – she can give Joseph a kiss before she goes if she likes. At the end of the carol, once people have sat down the figures stir again.)

Angel	What's happened? Where's Mary gone?
Joseph	I told you, lad. They've taken her off to the stable in the prayer corner. This time of year, lad, you have to think outside the box. They'll take me next.
Angel	Why?
Joseph	Because I come next in the story. We were engaged you see, but when I found out that she was expecting a baby, folk thought it was a scandal, you see. And I thought maybe I'd better break it off, quietly like.
Angel	And did you?
Joseph	No, lad. That's where you came in.
Angel	I did?
Joseph	You came to me in a dream and told me that it was God's baby and Mary had been

178

good as gold. So I made a promise that I'd bring him up as my own, and teach him my trade.

Angel   And what happened then?

Joseph   Then we went to Bethlehem.

Angel   Why? That's a bit hard on Mary, travelling when she's …..you know.

Joseph   It was the law, lad. You can't argue with the emperor. That's what he'd ordered.

Balthazar I say, you two. Cave*! Freeze. Someone's coming.

(All the characters freeze in their positions.)

READING: Luke Chapter 2 vv 1 – 7

CAROL: O little town of Bethlehem

SCENE 4:
(During the carol Joseph goes off behind the chancel – shaking hands with the Angel before he goes. The shepherds get out of the box. At the end of the carol, once people have sat down, the figures stir again, apart from Shepherd 4 who stays sleeping.)

Shepherd I   Right then. Are we all here? Where's Simon? Wake him up someone. *(Shepherd*

---

* *Cave is pronounced cay-vee and is Latin for 'watch out' – very popular in a certain sort of private school slang.*

3 gives him a shake and he gets up as the dialogue goes on.)
Everyone got their kit from last year? Sticks? Crooks? Sheepskins?

Angel   Who are you lot?.... You look a bit...rustic.

Shep 2   No need to get sniffy with us, Sunny Jim. We're the shepherds. We're very important in the story. We're witnesses. Your job is to come and tell us that the baby's been born.

Shep 1   Aye, there we are on the hills above Bethlehem minding t'sheep.

Shep 2   And our own businesses.

Shep 1   And up you pop. Lots of you. The whole heavenly host. Angels all over the sky.

Angel   Where are the others then?

Shep 1   Oh, they've only ever had one of you here.
[And the box of cherubs. They get packed away in cotton wool. More fragile – see. Someone had better go and wake them up too. *(Shepherd 3 or 4 goes to do this and lifts them out of the box. They come and sit round the shepherds' feet.)*]

Shep 2   And you tell us all t' leave sheep and go to Bethlehem and see t'babby.

Shep 1	*(Putting on a posh accent.)* And see this thing which has come to pass….
Shep 2	You're harking back there, lad. They don't put it like that these days.
Shep 1	More's the pity. So they take us off to the stable and arrange us tastefully and adoringly.
Shep 2	*(Meaningfully.)* When we don't fall sideways on top of each other.
Shep 1	That weren't my fault, that time. Someone put me on a lump of straw.
Angel	*(Eagerly, breaking into what looks as though it might turn into a row.)* So I come with you this time.
Shep 1	Nay, lad. Tha's still got work to do.
Angel	*(Crestfallen.)* Oh, I say….
Shep 2	Watch out! Someone's coming.

(All the characters freeze in their positions.)

READING: *Luke Chapter 2 vv 8 – 16*

CAROL: *While shepherds watched their flocks*
SCENE 5:
(During the carol the Shepherds [and cherubs] go off to behind the chancel. The wise men get themselves out of the box.)

Balthazar	Now then. Are we all ready? Dear me. This year we are a *little* the worse for wear. It's high time they repainted us. Eastern sages, kings…we look more like a bunch of strolling players. We do have some standards to keep up.
Angel	Excuse me. Where do you fit into the story, and where do I come in?
Balthazar	You may well ask. We are *another* part of the story. Another set of people who come to see the baby. We, dear boy, are from the wider world. This wasn't just a little rustic incident, dear me, no. This was an event of cosmic significance.
Angel	*(Who thinks he has got the hang of it by now.)* So I tell you all about the baby?
Balthazar	*(Crushingly.)* No.
Angel	But I tell everyone else.
Balthazar	Indeed you do, dear boy. But not us. We, my dear, have a star. And we can read the heavens. We are scholars.
Angel	*(Flattened.)* So you don't need me…
Balthazar	Indeed we do. You come and warn us of the danger *after* we see the baby, so that we all get away safely, including the baby.
Angel	The danger! I thought that this was a

happy story.

Balthazar   Indeed it is, dear boy. But like all stories with happy endings, there is peril and sadness on the way. In this story there is a wicked king who will kill the baby if he finds out where he is.

Angel   Our baby?

Balthazar   Indeed, yes. Our baby. The light of the world. That's where you come in.
Don't look so downcast, dear boy. They always bring you out of the box last, you and the baby.

Angel   So we come to the stable too?

Balthazar   Indeed you do. You can't have Christmas without the baby. Come to that, you can't have Christmas without the angels.
That's the whole point you see. God with us. That's what makes the humans come alive too.
Now do be a good chap and shut up. Someone's coming.

(They freeze for the reading. Then during the carol the kings and their entourage go off to the stable leaving the Angel alone on stage.)

READING: *Matthew Chapter 2 vv 1 – 12*

CAROL: *In the bleak midwinter*

Angel: *(Who has been rummaging among the newspaper in the box.)* They've all gone. I expect they'll be coming soon for me. I can't wait to get to the stable.
(To the congregation) I expect you feel like that too. You can come too, I think. Just as soon as they've put me in the right place. Oh, and the baby. He's the most important. You can't have Christmas without him, that much I do know. He's its living heart. But I've looked everywhere for him. He's not in the box. I'm not sure where they put him away last year. I'm not sure what I ought to do.
(Comes down into the congregation.)
I know, please, do you think that I could borrow your baby?
(Takes baby from woman in congregation and goes out to the back of the Chancel.)

INVITATION to the congregation to come to the stable with their gifts for the Children's Society

Prayer over the Christingles and offerings
Carol sung by children: Away in a Manger
Christingle prayer

FINAL CAROL
Blessing

Righteous Joseph

There aren't many carols in the hymnbooks about Joseph, but this is an old traditional one, shortened for the occasion:

When righteous Joseph wedded was
To Israel's Hebrew maid,
The angel Gabriel came from heaven
And to the Virgin said;
'Hail, blessed Mary, full of grace,
The Lord remain on thee;
Thou shalt conceive and bear a son
Our Saviour for to be.

Then Joseph thought to shun all shame
And Mary to forsake;
But God's dear angel in a dream
His mind did undertake:
"Fear not, old Joseph, she's thy wife,
She's still a spotless maid;
There's no conceit or sin at all
Against her can be laid."

Then Mary and her husband kind
Together did remain,
Until the time of Jesus' birth,
As scripture doth make plain.
Sing praises all, both young and old,
To him that wrought such things;
And all without the means of man
Sent us the King of kings,

Then sing you all, both great and small,
Nowell, Nowell, Nowell!
We may rejoice to hear the voice,
Of the angel Gabriel.

Sing to the tune Tyrol, repeating second half of tune for chorus at the end.

Lightning Source UK Ltd.
Milton Keynes UK
UKOW03f0444211014

240409UK00002B/35/P